Contents

D0003337

Introduction by the author

This work is not a historical treatise in the scholarly sense — it is 'oral history'.

This is the account my grandmother (1867–1957) gave me of her ancestors, everything that lived on in her own memory and, in addition, what her own mother (1831–1913) and her grandmother (1797–1877) had told her at the time when she was only a child and a young girl. These women were truly committed to the traditional oral transmission of history. The final chapter is an account of my mother (1890–1975), partly from her reports and partly from my own memories. They are primarily stories I wanted to retain for my children, because they urged me, time and again, to write it all down. Episode followed episode, just as they were present in my mind. Eventually, I decided to collect the fragments and describe the world in which these four women lived their lives. I knew the historical and social context fairly well from documents which I had accumulated over many years about past life in the Engadin and the Val Bregaglia. My notes turned into a chronicle which may be of interest to others, too.

Some old photographs, reproduced throughout the book, may be helpful in filling out these memories.

A part of the history of people who live in our mountains is reproduced in this way, but in the sense with which Hans Saner introduced Karl Jasper's autobiography: 'You do not experience what has happened, but rather the constant presence of what happened in the past, and only as an impression, as another sort of poetry.'

Foreword to the English edition

Marcella Maier (1920–2018)

The author, Marcella Maier, was a journalist and author or co-author of several books. Her interests were wide: they included local history, tourism, women's issues, the environment and social history.

Marcella was born in St Moritz, Switzerland, in 1920. She went to primary and secondary school there and graduated with a diploma, specialising in business and commercial subjects. After periods in Geneva and in Italy, to improve her foreign language skills, she worked in the hospitality and retail sectors. During the war years she was enrolled to work on farms as part of her mandatory 'Landdienst' service and she volunteered in the women's section of the Swiss army. She then worked as an administrative secretary with the 'Kur- und Verkehrsverein St. Moritz', the official organisation responsible for tourism in the region.

She married Duri Maier in 1947 and during the following nine years they had four daughters. In addition to her duties as a housewife and mother, Marcella supported her husband in his workshop. She also started working as a journalist and this was eventually to become her full-time career later on. She wrote for German and Romansh radio stations and her work was published in newspapers and magazines in both languages.

Marcella Maier did not only show a great interest in politics, but she was very much politically engaged. In 1972, she became the first woman member of the 'St. Moritzer

Gemeinderat' (the equivalent of a local council), and was elected to the 'Bündner Grosse Rat' (the equivalent of the parliament of the Canton of Grisons). This is all the more remarkable because Swiss women only gained the right to vote in federal elections in February 1971.

In her family saga, *The green silk shawl*, the author provides a wealth of background information on the cultural and economic history, and on the details of the daily life in the Engadin and the Val Bregaglia from the end of the 18th to the beginning of the 21st centuries. It is a fascinating autobiographical oral history.

Throughout her long life, Marcella was committed to women's rights and actively supported many charitable and cultural causes. Although her failing eyesight was a personal sadness, she remained up-to-date with events in the outside world by listening to audio books and the radio. Just like the women she described in *The green silk shawl,* her own daughters and their families ensured that she could live as independently as possible until her death in July 2018. To quote the death announcement:

'Full of the joys of life, she went on a Sunday walk — two days later, she did not wake up.'

Alma 1797–1877

The priest had gone. Alma realised it as soon as she entered the kitchen in the morning. Everything was just as it had been on every other morning in the past two years — both kettles had been filled, and the wood on the hearth had been arranged in a way that she only needed to light the fire — and yet, something told her: Don Gerolamo was no longer there. Alma stayed still and looked around. What was it? She could not explain it. Slowly, she went into the anteroom, which was half open towards the garden. She had not been wrong. The bundle of Don Gerolamo's liturgical objects, carefully wrapped in a black cloth, was no longer there.

He had always got up very early, extracted the jug, chalice and the cloths from the bundle and arranged everything on the shelf. Then he celebrated Mass by himself, crossed the garden to fill Alma's kettles in the stream and carried them back to the kitchen, where he prepared the fire. First, he brushed the ash into the old bowl, which he put outside. After that, he carefully arranged some dry twigs, on which he placed the few thin pieces of wood, which he had already prepared the evening before, crosswise. On the top, he put the rougher logs and as soon as a match touched this elaborate tower, a cheerful fire flared up. He performed these tasks with a sort of quiet deference; Alma only lit the fireplace to prepare lunch.

Don Gerolamo then left the house, breviary in hand, walked along the brook all the way down to the footbridge and, having crossed over, walked up into the forest, where he prayed for an hour. Only then did he return to sit down for breakfast with Alma at the freshly scrubbed wooden table.

Alma, too, got up early, but Gerolamo was always up and about long before dawn. They consumed their rye bread in silence, sometimes with a piece of hard cheese, and drank a cup of goat's milk.

Alma stood in the vestibule for a while, lost in thought, before she entered the house again. The familiar kitchen suddenly appeared strange and empty to her. She opened the door to the adjacent storeroom. The spinning wheel was in the corner, with a silk shawl on its cross piece and, next to it, a letter. She opened it and read the few lines: Gerolamo thanked her for giving him shelter for nearly two years. He wrote that the time had now come for him to go to the people who needed his help and advice. His spinning wheel and his mother's shawl were his gifts to her.

Alma picked up the shawl. She had not seen it before. She wondered whether he had kept it with the liturgical objects — it was made of the most beautiful silk. Gold-coloured ornaments had been woven into the green background and a delicate fringed border finished off the hem. Alma slowly unfolded the shawl, held the pretty cloth to her cheek and then placed it on her head. She went into the kitchen and looked at herself in the small, blurry mirror. It did, indeed, look good on her thick chestnut hair. What would people say if she wore it on Sundays? Alma threw her head back with a softly mocking smile. There would no doubt be whispering. She knew only too well that there was gossip about her — she, a young widow, who now shared a house with a man. This alone caused a stir — but that this man was a Catholic priest in this exclusively Protestant valley was outrageous and earned her pointed comments and disapproval.

When Alma thought of that, she shrugged her shoulders. It had, after all, been the same with her mother when Don Gerolamo had lived with them. He had arrived in the Val Bregaglia as a refugee and her parents had provided a home for him. In those days her father had still been alive, but the terrible years among the foreign troops had taken their toll on his health. He was already very weak at that time and died in the subsequent very cold winter.

People had probably expected that the priest would leave the house at that time. He stayed until spring, however, a fact that provided ample food for gossip. Just as had happened with Alma now, he abruptly returned to Italy, only to find himself on the run again a few years later, and again living in her mother's house in Soglio for a longer period of time.

Alma helped, like the other children in the village, with work at home — both in the house and in the field; but even when she was still at school, during the summer, she worked as a day labourer for other families, especially for Signora Clementina down in Bondo. She and her husband Corrado, who was a number of years older, had no children. He was a saddler and repaired the tack of the many horses that passed by. There was a lot of traffic in the Val Bregaglia, which was a regular transit route to the much frequented mountain passes of Septimer, Maloja and Julier: many horse carts and trains of pack mules[1] used the road. It was therefore not surprising that torn straps and ropes, loops and buckles had to be replaced as quickly as possible to allow men and horses to proceed the next day. This meant that Clementina, too, had to help in the workshop and therefore she relied on help in the house as well as in the smallholding and the large garden. As she had lived in Italy for many years, she taught Alma many new skills, for example preparing wonderful

---

[1] The original German word is 'Saumkolonne', which is unusual, and closest to the old English expression 'sumpter convoy'.

Italian dishes that were quite different from the simple cuisine of the valley.

After several years in the house of Corrado and Clementina, she met the man who would later become her husband. Giovanni, the son of a family who had immigrated from Italy, had been born in Siena and spoke the beautiful Italian of Tuscany. Although he understood the dialect of the Val Bregaglia, he was not fluent and some people in the village interpreted this as arrogance. Because of his bad health, he had come to the Val Bregaglia to live with his father's sister, his Aunt Clementina. Giovanni was good with his hands and learnt very quickly how to use awl and yarn. He soon proved to be a capable assistant for Corrado. Apart from the leather gear needed by the farmers and the passing tradesmen, Giovanni also produced beautifully crafted bags and pouches, which sold at a good price. Unfortunately, his health continued to give him trouble, and he was often unwell.

Alma was already over thirty when she married Giovanni. Her uncle and aunt allowed them to live in a small extension to their house, which had been added towards the mountainside. It consisted of a kitchen with fireplace and sleeping quarters above it, as well as a storeroom with an additional small chamber and a wooden shed, which served as a stable.

Her marriage to Giovanni brought Alma unexpected happiness, for he was a kind and sensitive husband, who introduced her to the beauty of his language and the world of books.

After two years they had a little daughter, Lisabetta. They were a small, contented family. Giovanni, however, was increasingly afflicted with a cough. His breath was laboured, he lost weight, and ten months after Lisabetta's birth, he died. Consumption, it was said.

Alma was on her own now. She continued to work for her husband's relatives — ever more frequently, as Corrado and Clementina began to grow infirm with old age. If there was any spare time with all these duties, she helped other women with their cleaning and washing, particularly when they all did their laundry at the village fountain.

Alma shoved the silk shawl, folded into a tiny bundle, into her pocket and turned her attention to the spinning wheel. She took hold of the spokes — a gentle push was enough — and the wheel nimbly whirred round and round. It was a particularly good spinning wheel, much easier to handle than the heavier wheels that were used down in the valley. In contrast to these, it was exquisitely crafted, decorated with chip carvings coloured red, which stood out prettily against the dark green of the rest of the woodwork.

The beautiful spinning wheel had been in Don Gerolamo's possession when he had first looked for a refuge with Alma's mother up in Soglio, over a year previously, but in vain — she had already died, and other people now lived in the house. He had then asked after Alma and was referred to Bondo. Just like her mother before her, Alma had not made a fuss, but simply opened her door for him, unconcerned about people gossiping. He told her that he had had to flee, but without going into details. And Alma had not asked any questions.

She had later learnt — from people travelling past who had come to Corrado's workshop — that he had been accused of disregarding the Roman Catholic dogma and that he had not obeyed the orders of the Church hierarchy, which resulted in his exclusion from the priesthood and all priestly activities. It was said that, by escaping, he avoided the punishments that he would have had to expect.

His post had been in isolated mountain villages on Lake Como, and as far as the unpretentious, hard-working population there was concerned, he was still their pastor: every now and then he disappeared for a few days. Rumour had it that he walked on hidden trails to his parishes to celebrate Mass — in secret — in small, remote chapels. And afterwards, he returned to the Val Bregaglia on secret paths, weighed down by the gifts of the poor farmers: dried meat, cheese, eggs, polenta.

These staples helped to supplement Alma's meagre earnings. It was obvious that Don Gerolamo did not want to be a burden for the widow, though he did not, of course, have an income himself. However, he was able to spin the wool from Alma's sheep like nobody else, to such a fine and smooth yarn. The fact that a man was spinning wool was unusual and he was mocked in the village, though the best spinners had to admit, not without envy, that they were not able to produce such soft, silky and thin threads of wool.

He left the finished balls with Alma, who could sell them at a good price, because the wool spun by the priest was in demand, and many a woman brought him her wool to be spun. The pay for this work also went towards household expenses, ensuring that Don Gerolamo's stay in her house was not a strain on Alma.

Alma looked at the shelves, which took up one wall of the storeroom. On the top plank there were the neatly arranged balls of wool from her sheep, and on the lower planks those which had yet to be collected by the women in the village.

Don Gerolamo had shown Alma how to spin such fine yarn, how to tread the foot board regularly and not too fast, and how the bundle of wool had to slide through the fingers so that the thread was not too stiff but was, at the same time, twisted in a way that it did not tear easily. She had learnt and practised, but felt that she was not succeeding as well as Don Gerolamo. Nevertheless, her yarn was valued as much as the priest's by the village women.

Don Gerolamo helped with other tasks as well; for example, looking after her goat and the sheep. When he went into the forest, he returned with dead branches and kindling, and there was always enough firewood to cook. He lived in the low, unheated chamber above the open storeroom, which could only be reached from the garden via an external staircase. When he was in the house, he sat in the kitchen at the spinning wheel, working in silence. Little Lisabetta sat, when she was not asleep, next to him on the floor and played with the animals that Gerolamo had carved for her from branches and twigs. They all had their meals together, including the child. There was not much talk. Everyone was lost in their own thoughts.

The malicious insinuations about her and the priest were not mentioned. Just as Don Gerolamo adhered to his clerical commitments, he also fulfilled his pledges. And Alma had her own pride. This man was a guest in her house, a member of the clergy and she respected him, although he belonged to a different denomination, about which she did not know and understand a lot. People might say and think what they wanted to — she stuck to the principles she had learnt from childhood and did not pay any attention to the gossip.

Lisabetta's plaintive voice interrupted Alma's thoughts and she climbed up the stairs to pick up the child so that they could have breakfast together. While drinking her milk,

Lisabetta suddenly pointed to the empty chair and asked, 'Where is Lamo?' This was what she called the priest, for she could not yet pronounce his difficult name.

'Yes, where might he be? Where had he gone?' Alma tried to imagine which path he could have chosen. It was, after all, not the first time that he had disappeared for some time, but he had always returned after a short while. This time it was different. The letter made that clear. Might he have found shelter somewhere else, with people who were well disposed towards him? Or had he perhaps confronted his superiors and stuck defiantly to his own position? Had he put himself in danger with this reaction? Alma began to realise that she was worried about him. He was a good man — that she had learnt — but probably someone who did not easily submit to a yoke. She could only hope that he managed to both stick to his principles and keep the office of priest in his parishes.

The winter after the priest's departure was terrible. It was freezing for weeks and the cold was worse when the sun did not rise above the high peaks of the Sciora and Badile mountains. In the frigid shadows of the steep rock faces, the chill crept into the walls and into the houses, and no warming fire could drive it out. Many villagers were not sufficiently prepared for such a long and intense period of cold, and their wood reserves did not last, however thriftily the inhabitants used them. In addition, the chestnut harvest had been bad in the autumn, and chestnuts were the main staple food of the population in the valley. This shortage was felt in all houses, but particularly in Alma's. She, too, had not been able to collect enough wood. It was impossible for Alma, holding the hand of the now three-year-old Lisabetta, to forage for wood in the steep forests, and nor was it feasible to carry home heavy burdens.

Food stocks were also short. Corrado had died in the autumn and his wife Clementina had survived him only by a few months. Alma had thus lost her place of work. It turned out to be impossible to find another job in the middle of winter, as all work in the fields had stopped and also, in effect, most of the traffic across the mountain passes. In order to make sure Lisabetta did not have to go without food, Alma often missed dinner herself and went to bed hungry. If the grocer over in Promontogno had not been such a charitable man, the situation would no doubt have been even worse.

The shop had been in the same family for generations and the owners had become reasonably affluent as a result. The current owner, Gaudenzio, was known throughout the valley for his generosity towards the poor. He jotted down their modest purchases in a notebook and waited patiently until they were able to settle what they owed. This way, he rarely suffered a loss, for those in need felt that their honour was at stake. Alma used to pay for her shopping with the money she earned from spinning and from selling the wool from her sheep. After Corrado's and Clementina's deaths she, too, was forced to take credit from Gaudenzio. Alma found this hard to swallow and her thoughts centred solely around the fact that life could not go on in this way — she did not want to live through another winter like this.

The previous months had been nearly as horrendous as the winter when they had to escape the French — or had it been the Austrians or the Russians? Alma remembered that time only vaguely, but even now, years afterwards, it was spoken about in terms of terror. Foreign troops had marched through the valley. There was talk of 'the Emperor's army' and 'the French army', and even of soldiers from Russia.

The heavily armed forces marched up the valley, only to promptly return again from Maloja not long afterwards, hotly pursued by units of the enemy's army. They chased each other away. Depending on the fortunes of war, the expelled headed back and chased away those who had previously banished them. They all, however, pillaged, plundered and looted: they took people's livestock, food, hay and firewood, their shoes, their leather and, of course, all money and valuables.

Alma had been very young at that time and was not able to distinguish between her own, personal experiences and what she had heard older people talk about when they shared reminiscences of the horrors.

She vividly remembered the day when there had been great excitement in Soglio. The inhabitants had run over to the open country, to the east of the village, from where they could look down into the valley. Men in colourful uniforms passed along the road — with flashing guns, horse carts pulling strange two-wheeled iron vehicles carrying weird pipes, screams reverberated, and harsh orders were heard. No human being could be seen outdoors down in Bondo, no animal in the fields. All doors and windows were locked and bolted. But the soldiers pushed open the gates and one could see the people fleeing out of their back doors up into the forest.

More than once, the population of Soglio witnessed such events from their high location and each time they trembled at the thought of invaders coming up to their village and wreaking such destruction there, but fortunately it was situated at an altitude way above the valley.

The strongest memories were of the weeks spent in the middle of the winter in one of the huts that belonged to the mountain hamlet,[2] which was normally only used in the summer. Many people, mostly women and children, had moved up from Castasegna to Soglio, and they were bursting with terrible news. Everything was being stolen; 'requisitioned' was the term. The men were apparently forced to serve the officers and soldiers, and they had to slaughter their own cattle for the military kitchens. No woman was safe from this rampant mob of soldiers. In panic, the frightened people pushed further up into the woods. Soglio, too, would no longer be safe, if all houses in the valley had been looted.

Therefore, the men in Soglio had also ordered the women to escape with the children to the huts high up on the mountain. Alma had never forgotten those days and nights, the terrible cold and the darkness. In the corner of the shack, the villagers prepared a sort of camp bed for the children on a pile of straw, and then covered them up to their necks with everything they could find — old blankets, sacks and material normally used to collect hay from the fields. They were lying in the dark, tightly pressed together, frightened and very hungry, because the little food they had been able to take on their rushed flight had soon been used up. Although some of the fathers managed to come up secretly during the night, bringing with them anything edible they had been able to get hold of, it was not always possible to find food nor to bring it up to the mountains.

These years of war and starvation had become deeply entrenched in the folk memory, and people talked about the events they had experienced then, again and again.

---

[2] The Swiss term for such a hamlet is 'Maiensäss'. 'Mai' means 'May', 'säss' is 'seat'. A Maiensäss is a collection of huts very high up in the mountains used for grazing cows from spring until autumn.

Bondo towards the Bondasca Glacier
Engraving by Ludwig Rohbock, before 1861

At last the winter was over. The sun climbed again over the high rocky towers and peaks and poured its warmth into the narrow valley. In the meadows surrounding the village there were the first signs of green, and towards the evening deer came out of the forest and grazed near the row of small hay barns on the flat ground to the west of the church.

An indescribable feeling of relief and hope permeated people just as the bright sunrays did. Alma had opened the windows and doors of her little house in order to get rid of the cold and humidity. On a day like this, one should not stay in the house, she thought. She packed all the balls of wool she had spun over the last few weeks into a cloth, took Lisabetta's hand and together they wandered over to Promontogno.

The stream had swollen massively with the meltwater and roared underneath them when they crossed the bridge. The wagtails hopped from stone to stone on the bank, and in the chestnut trees near the caves, the chaffinches blared out their joy of spring into the pleasantly warm spring air. The jays were performing their wedding dances above the old fir trees in the steep meadows behind the village. In rapid flight they spiralled up and up into the air only to plunge down abruptly like a stone. A little above the ground, they caught themselves and promptly started rising again.

Lisabetta trotted along cheerfully, singing her own tunes, and pointed to the first flowers; coltsfoot, on the embankment, crocuses and daisies in the meadows, and cinquefoil at the edge of the path. On the other side of the valley, in between the bare beech trunks, there was a scattering of wild cherry trees in bloom and, next to the little walls along the side of the path, blackthorn had adorned itself with bright blossoms.

In the garden of Gaudenzio the grocer, incredibly, the pear tree was already in bloom, and among the beds, cowslips and March bells were nodding in the early wind of spring.

Gaudenzio took the wool that Alma had produced and removed the little booklet from the drawer in which he had noted the amount Alma had spun for him and what groceries she had received from him. He carefully entered the numbers, and then calculated — there was still a small debt that Alma owed. She had hoped so much that everything she had chalked up could be wiped off completely, and she was now disappointed that, despite all her efforts, she was still in Gaudenzio's debt.

He felt for her. Pushing his glasses further up his forehead, he remarked, 'Do not worry. You are not the only one in this position. After this winter, it is hardly surprising. I know that you will pay up as soon as you can. It is not much anymore, after all, so do not let this matter spoil this beautiful day.'

'Thank you. I do not know how I would have survived the last few months if you had not given me credit. My child would have gone hungry, for sure.'

'But you did go hungry', the grocer thought to himself and looked at her silently.

She had, actually, been a strong woman, but now she was thin, and her cheeks were hollow. Without asking, he packed some corn and barley into her cloth. Alma tried to fend him off.

'No, I want to pay up for the rest first, before I buy anything else; you can rest assured that I shall get by.'

'Let go', Gaudenzio grumbled and added a chunk of cheese, 'Do not tell me that we cannot agree on this.'

Alma allowed him to proceed — the grain was more than welcome, as there was hardly any left in her house.

'Gaudenzio, I have another request. I have to find work. You are aware that there is nothing more to be done in Corrado and Clementina's house, and whatever little else there is in the village is simply not enough. Even though the two of us' — she pointed to Lisabetta — 'live very modestly. If you hear of anything, please think of me. You meet lots of people in your shop and you could perhaps ask some of them.'

'Of course. I will think of it. There will definitely be more work towards summer, and I am sure that I shall find something for you.'

Alma left the shop grateful and full of hope. Instead of returning home via shortest route, she took the path along the river and walked in a wide arc through the meadows. She picked grasses and flowers with Lisabetta and threw stones into the stream so that the water splashed up high, much to the child's delight, and they played hide and seek near the huts by entrance to the village.

A week later, when Alma was washing the laundry of a sick neighbour, Alberto, who ran the sawmill in the village, walked past and said, 'Gaudenzio has asked me to tell you that you should drop by.'

Alma was surprised. 'Did he not say anything else?'

'No, nothing.' Alberto was a man of few words.

She rinsed the laundry fast and carried it behind her house, where there was a washing line between the eaves and the walnut tree on the riverbank. In a great hurry, she hung up the sheets, the kitchen towels and the underwear. She did not even take time to cook lunch, but just sat herself and Lisabetta down for bread, cheese and milk, in order to go to Gaudenzio in Promontogno as soon as possible.

When she entered the grocer's, Gaudenzio looked up from his work. Alma immediately realised that he had good news for her.

'Signora Anna in the Palazzo in Soglio is looking for help. Plinio, who works on the farm, was here yesterday and mentioned it. I thought of you at once.'

'That would be great — but do you believe I would be good enough for this lady?'

'Alma — you are hard-working, you know that yourself. I shall recommend you. When Plinio comes tomorrow, I shall give him a few lines for the Signora. Apart from that, you speak High German, which she will appreciate. Go up as soon as you can and introduce yourself.'

'Good, in that case, I shall go the day after tomorrow.'

Two days later, Alma made her way up to Soglio in her Sunday best, holding Lisabetta's hand. To begin with, the little one bravely marched along with her short legs, but after thirty minutes, not unexpectedly, she started asking how much further it was going to be. Alma could not but agree to a break on the terrace near Plaz, where the 'cascine'[3], the old huts used for storing and drying chestnuts, stood under the trees. Sitting on a rock, they rested and ate the last dried chestnuts, which Alma had been able to save. Dried chestnuts had to be kept in the mouth for a while, until they were soft, and then one could chew them and enjoy their delicate, sweet taste.

Entranced, Alma looked around. There were green shoots and blossoms everywhere; the earth producing new food for humans and animals. On the way home, she would dig out dandelions to make a salad. With an egg — the hens had fortunately also started laying again — that would make

---

[3] A 'cascina' (Italian) is a farmhouse.

a good meal. Near some of the huts, the wild spinach had begun to show its first leaves and in a week's time she could come back to collect spinach.

She sighed with relief — surely the worst was now over. And if the matter of a position with Signora Anna was successful, the future would be brighter, too.

The two took up their path again, as it wound its way towards the mountains with many bends. The white church steeple of Soglio emerged further up between two tall poplars and they soon arrived. Alma stood still and looked at the houses, which stood next to each other in a tight row. The roofs, which were made of heavy stone slabs, and the grey façades, were bathed in the gleaming light of the spring sun, in contrast to the dark brown timber on the upper floors. How well she knew every house, every stable and every garden. It was the village of her childhood. There was still a lot of snow — glistening like silver — on the mountains across the valley from which the striking ridges and spires of the Bondasca Range protruded into the blue sky. She strode along the lane to the village entrance where granite had been added to the cobblestones to make access for horse-drawn carts easier.

Having pulled the outside bell firmly, she walked hesitantly through the gate of the Palazzo Battista — a grand structure, whose elegant architecture, with its bright windows and outbuildings surrounding a courtyard, was evidence of the power and wealth of the von Salis family. She found herself in a hall with a high, domed ceiling; there were doors on both sides and a staircase at the end.

An old woman rushed down the steps. Alma knew her. It was Caterina, who had been in service in the Palazzo even when Alma was still a child.

When she heard why Alma had come, she looked cold and reserved. Rather reluctantly, she bid Alma to follow her. As they reached the upper floor, Alma looked around astonished: the hall spread over two floors. There were weapons, suits of armour and portraits of very formal gentlemen.

Caterina vanished through a narrow door, but reappeared at once and indicated to Alma that she should follow her, throwing a suspicious look at Lisabetta. The child had observed everything quietly and now shyly snuggled up to her mother, as they stood in the bright room in front of Signora Anna. This slim lady, whose delicate, aristocratic face was framed by light, partly greying, hair, sat in an armchair near the window with a book in her hand.

'So, you are Alma. Gaudenzio recommended you to me. I hear that you are a widow and have worked for Corrado and Clementina. I knew the two well — good people.'

Her duties, Signora Anna explained, would consist in giving a helping hand to Caterina with all the chores, as she had grown too old to cope with all the work in this big household by herself. There might be problems, however, because Caterina would perhaps not be able to get used to the fact that she was no longer in charge of everything on her own. As was so often the case with the elderly, she would find it hard to hand over some of her duties. Alma would have to be patient and make sure that the old servant did not feel that she was being pushed aside.

'I have known Caterina since I was a child, and I shall certainly get on with her. Indeed, I have been working a lot with old people over the past few years', Alma explained.

'Is this your child? What is your name?' The Signora turned to Lisabetta. The little one remained silent and only after a nudge from her mother, did she quietly utter her name.

'Lisabetta, that is also my name; Anna Elisabeth. How old are you?'

Lisabetta held up four fingers, without saying a word, and the Signora smiled. 'Let us say, then, this means that you are four years old and no doubt a well-behaved little girl who gives her mother pleasure.'

With this, she addressed Alma. 'What is the situation with the child? Can you have her with you while you are at work or what were your plans?'

'Lisabetta is a quiet girl and fortunately she can very easily entertain herself. In addition, I think she is now old enough to be with the other children in the village. If I were ever held up because of her, however, I would catch up on my work in the evening. In any case, my work would not suffer, I assure you.'

This was said in a firm and positive tone, and the Signora smiled.

'I believe you. You speak High German; where have you learnt that?'[4] Alma told her about her husband and that they had always communicated in the 'vera lingua'.[5]

---

[4] The Signora had expected Alma to address her in the local Swiss German dialect. High German would only be used in the written form, on very formal occasions or to communicate with people who were not Swiss German. High German was, and still is, taught to all children in Swiss German areas, when they start primary school.

[5] Alma's husband Giovanni had been born in Siena and was a native Italian speaker — she mentions the 'beautiful Tuscan Italian' he spoke and the fact that he understood the local dialect of the Val Bregaglia, but that he did not speak it well and that they therefore communicated in High German.

'I am very happy about this', the Signora said, adding, 'You can move into a room overlooking the garden, and as far as your wages go, I shall set them in line with the current standard — after I have made the necessary enquiries.'

Alma was happy with this, and she also agreed to start as soon as possible.

A few days later, Alma and Lisabetta moved in with their sparse belongings and Alma started her job. There was enough work in the rambling four-storey house with its corridors and staircases and the great number of rooms, even though only few of them were inhabited. Nevertheless, they needed to be aired every now and then, and they had to be kept clean.

Caterina was very reserved towards Alma at first, but was nonetheless glad of her help and increasingly entrusted her with housework and cleaning tasks. The only tasks she would not leave for Alma were serving Signora Anna and looking after her room.

Garden work, too, was soon part of Alma's duties, as it became more and more burdensome for the old woman, though a young man from the village, whose father had already looked after the Palazzo garden, came in several times a week to maintain the magnificent grounds, which had been laid out in the French style. There were yew hedges surrounding rose beds, brightly flowering peonies, fruit trees and two tall, unusual, redwood trees. When necessary, Alma helped him, and she was also responsible for the upkeep of the vegetable beds in the north-east corner at the foot of the steeply ascending, rocky hillside.

The big, domed kitchen remained part of Caterina's empire, but she allowed Alma to help her with the stove. Alma knew how to make herself useful without being intrusive. She always allowed Caterina to allocate work for her, helped her when she wanted her to do so, asked her advice and followed her orders in such a way that Caterina soon gave up her negative attitude and good team work started to develop between them.

Signora Anna quickly realised that this was the case and was glad that Alma managed to handle her loyal, old maid so skilfully, particularly in view of the fact that in the past there had often been unpleasant friction with young helpers.

Alma settled in quickly. Lisabetta obviously liked living in the Palazzo, too. While Alma worked, the child played in the entrance hall or on the sunny forecourt. With her quiet manner, she had also won the heart of Caterina, who was only too happy to let her sit in the kitchen with her, at the end of the long table, playing with a pan and a wooden spoon. In the garden, too, Lisabetta was allowed to play with the long cones of the redwood trees and with pebbles, sometimes even when Signora Anna strolled along the gravel-covered paths with her silk sun umbrella.

One morning, with dawn still in the alleyways, Alma set out from Giuliano's house across the village square and ran hurriedly along the narrow lane to the backdoor of the Palazzo. Quietly, so as not to wake up Lisabetta, she entered her room. Lisabetta was not there. The bed was empty. The shock that hit the mother paralysed her completely. She could barely breathe. Wild fear enveloped her. Where was the child? She ran out to the staircase, through all the corridors and called her little one in desperation. She was nowhere.

Soglio, view from the east
Coloured steel engraving by Ludwig Rohbock, before 1861

Alma ran up the stairs and into Caterina's room; she was getting dressed and initially did not understand at all what was going on, why Alma was asking questions about Lisabetta, and why she was so agitated. Caterina knew nothing. In panic, Alma dashed into Signora Anna's chambers without knocking.

'Lisabetta…', she panted breathlessly.

The Signora sat bolt upright in her bed, and next to her was Lisabetta, sound asleep. Alma sank onto a chair and started to sob violently. She was shaking so badly that she barely managed to regain her breath. Lisabetta woke up, looked around in astonishment, then glanced at Signora Anna and Alma and began to cry, extending her arms towards her mother.

'Mummy, Mummy', she cried.

Alma jumped up and put her arms around her, still sobbing.

Signora Anna's face showed displeasure, even anger, and she said, in a severe tone, 'Where were you during the night? And leaving the child alone?'

In her confusion, Alma could only say, 'With Giuliano'. 'What do you mean, with Giuliano?' Signora Anna looked at her maid with a frown.

'Well, actually…no, with Giuliano's mother. She is ill. I was looking after her.'

Signora's face was a picture of surprise.

'So you keep vigil for the sick Celestina at night?' And after a pause she added, 'Lisabetta must have woken up and was probably afraid. Whatever it was, she screamed so loudly on the staircase that I woke up. I brought her to my room, but it took her a long time to calm down. I did not know, of course, where I could have found you.'

Alma lowered her head and muttered an apology.

'Go now and give Lisabetta her milk! We shall talk later.'

Still in a daze, Alma went down into the kitchen, where Caterina had already lit a fire in the hearth. She listened to Alma's tale of what had happened. She had not heard anything herself, but that was because she did not hear particularly well any more. Downcast, Alma prepared breakfast. What would happen if Signora were to dismiss her? It was only too obvious how indignant she was.

Alma knew how lucky she had been to get the position in the Palazzo. She loved her work and was only too glad that she could always have her child with her, and for this, she was immensely grateful to the Signora.

23

She could have been so happy, if the thought of winter had not been bothering her all the time. During the cold season, the Palazzo was closed. The high, vast rooms could not really be heated properly, despite the beautifully decorated tiled stoves. For this reason, Signora Anna and Caterina moved into the milder region of the Rhine valley — where the family had another castle — as soon as winter sent its first harbingers. This had always been the case and Alma had been aware of this when she took on the position.

She knew that she could hardly have found another, better position, but she was not able to stop herself thinking about the problem of the winter months without work and without a source of income. Given that there was no other opportunity to find casual work, even in the summer, it was clear that practically nobody would be looking for help in the winter, when the country was under a thick blanket of snow.

It was therefore clear for Alma that she had to plan ahead for the winter. She saved her wages tirelessly and tried not to touch what she had put aside once she had paid off her last debts to Gaudenzio. Granted, she was able to spin the wool from her sheep when they came down from the alp higher up in the mountains, but would that, together with her savings, be enough to survive the winter? In addition, Corrado's nephews had given her to understand that they, as rightful heirs, were intending to take over the little house in Bondo. Where should she and Lisabetta go in that case? There was no way for them to be able to stay in their room in the cold Palazzo without heating. During sleepless nights, Alma worried and could not think of a solution.

It seemed like a stroke of fate when her cousin, Giuliano, who lived across the village square opposite the Palazzo, asked her if she could help his wife with the care of his seriously ill mother by looking after the patient overnight every now and then.

At first, Alma hesitated. Could she leave Lisabetta alone at night? But the little girl always slept deeply and never had nightmares like other children. Increasingly, she had made friends with the other children of her age in the village and romped around the whole day — in the lanes and hay barns. She was allowed to join them when they went to the meadows, when the adults were busy harvesting in the fields. As a result, she was really exhausted in the evenings and always slept soundly through the night.

Alma therefore dared to agree to Giuliano's proposal. The nights with the sick patient were not easy. She was restless, in pain, and repeatedly had to be given cooling compresses. She was also often confused, wanting to get up and leave the room, and was difficult to calm down and take back to bed. As Alma was strong and healthy, she usually managed to return to sleep quickly on the narrow bed that had been put into the patient's room, so that her normal day job was not affected. In the evening, when everyone in the Palazzo was asleep, she crossed the village square to Giuliano's house and returned early in the morning to her room. When her patient woke her up, she often sneaked over to Lisabetta in order to check that the child was asleep.

Over the course of weeks her help was needed more often. Care during the day became so demanding that Alma was eventually taking over night duties completely. That, however, turned out to be a big challenge, particularly in high summer when there were many guests in the Palazzo, nephews and nieces and other relations from the various branches of the von Salis family. Meals were taken in the dining room on the ground floor, big pots and pans were steaming in the kitchen, beds had to be made and cart loads of bed and table linen had to be washed at the big covered fountain. After such busy days, Alma found it hard to look after Celestina at night, but she told herself again and again that the remuneration she received from Giuliano would come in useful during the winter.

How, though, should life continue after this incident? She was aware that it had not been right to leave the child alone without telling anyone about her nocturnal activities. On the other hand, what should she have done?

She ran over to Giuliano after lunch and told him quickly what had happened. He was concerned and felt guilty about the unfortunate situation. Alma was constantly thinking about it, trying to formulate an explanation that would clarify it all. She finally convinced herself that it would be best to be completely open about her circumstances.

Lisabetta did not leave her side all day, as if she was frightened that her mother would abandon her. Caterina said over dinner, 'You should go to the Signora afterwards.'

Alma's pulse was racing when she entered Signora Anna's rooms. Her mistress bid her sit down and said, 'I think we need to talk.'

Alma accepted that she should have come earlier and apologised.

'I love being here in the Palazzo and I enjoy the work and am very grateful to have this job, particularly because I can have my girl with me. We lack nothing, but I have to think of the winter, as you, Signora Anna, are going to leave Soglio and I shall not have any work then. I put my wages aside, untouched, but I am afraid my savings will not be enough for the winter. This is the reason why I am glad to get the small salary Giuliano pays me for the night vigils. I am also worried about accommodation. I assume that I cannot stay in the Palazzo over the winter and, though I am currently tolerated in the little house in Bondo, this will not be the case in the longer term. It is also near enough impossible to find any other kind of work over the winter. Apart from spinning my own wool and perhaps taking on some additional spinning jobs from one or two of the other families and, indeed, the night vigils, there are no other opportunities to earn money. Celestina is not going to live much longer, I suppose, and then that income will disappear as well.'

Signora Anna had listened to Alma in silence.

'I know that Giuliano's family needs your help urgently and I do not think you can let them down now. You should talk to Giuliano, however, and ask him whether he could rearrange the room next to the patient — Lisabetta could then sleep with you. It would probably not be good for her if she woke up again and found herself alone in a pitch-dark house. It would be best if you went over to Giuliano now and talked to him. I shall think about everything else and see what can be done.'

Alma, who had expected a reprimand and was now experiencing warm understanding was so relieved that she had to hold back her tears. In a choking voice, she expressed her gratitude and went off to Giuliano. It was obvious that he, too, was extremely relieved about the happy turn of events. The Signora's proposal was put into action and the little pantry next to the sickroom was emptied and a bed was moved in there.

Lisabetta, who had not got over the shock of the previous night, initially cried and fought against the unfamiliar room and the different bed. Alma therefore lay down beside her and pulled the child towards her under the cover, where she cuddled up to her mother and soon fell asleep.

The first pears ripened in the garden, and Alma took them up to the Signora in a bowl.

'Have a seat. I have thought about our discussion', she said. 'First of all, I am happy with your work. You work hard, and you are diligent and have good manners, and I appreciate that. In addition, you have understood how to live and work with my loyal Caterina. As far as I know, there have not been any conflicts between the two of you and that cannot always have been easy. I would like to be able to count on you next summer, too, and I have considered how this could be done. People have told me that you are particularly good at spinning and that your wool is more delicate and softer than that of other women. I suggest that you could spin the wool from all our sheep.'

'All your wool?' Anna asked surprised, as she pictured, in her mind, the large flock of sheep of the von Salis family.

'Yes, of course. You should also go into the Palazzo regularly and make sure that everything is in order. When I go away, you would scrub the whole house thoroughly, and that would no doubt take two weeks. In the spring, before I move back in, you would air the place and clean it again, because the dust settles on everything when an old house is left empty. You can then prepare the soil in the vegetable garden, too, and start sowing again. And you will certainly be able to do other bits and pieces before I return. I expect you to write down the hours you work, and then you will be paid. To help you get through the winter, I shall pay you part of your wages in advance.'

Alma got up and, thanking her, seized the Signora's hands.

'Something else', she said. 'We can let you have the fourth-floor room with the fireplace and the adjoining chamber in the south-western corner of the annex. You could move in there before the beginning of winter.'

Alma felt as if she were dreaming. A wave of joy flowed over her; to have a place to live and a solid income — that was more than she had dared dream.

When the forests turned colour and the chestnuts ripened, Signora Anna and Caterina left Soglio. Alma cleared the little house in Bondo, and Giuliano transported her handful of belongings with his horse and cart to her new lodgings in the tall house next to the Palazzo in Soglio. It gave her great pleasure to arrange the few pieces of furniture, household items and personal possessions in the two rooms. She put the spinning wheel next to the window and already imagined herself sitting there, busy spinning her mistress's wool, while snowflakes fell to the ground outside. With a feeling of reverence, she then unpacked the box with her late husband's books. She remembered the few rare hours when she was reading with Giovanni — those had been happy moments. She still did not have much time to read, but on a Sunday afternoon, when the work had been done, she liked to read and immerse herself in the wonderful world of the written word.

Lovingly, she put the silk shawl, which she had carefully kept in a leather case specially made by Giovanni all those years ago, on the top shelf of a closet. Furnished in this way, the humble but bright apartment, where even in winter the afternoon sun shone, turned into a cosy home for Alma and Lisabetta.

Nine winters had passed. Alma had sat at her spinning wheel every day, had spun all of her mistress's wool, while Lisabetta, who had learnt from her how to twist it into delicate and flexible yarn, had helped her diligently. Indeed, she had been able to take on additional spinning jobs. She did not have her own wool any more, as she had sold her sheep after the first summer in the Palazzo, because she did not have a shed where the sheep could have stayed over winter. Often people called on her to look after the sick and help with their care. She was said to have 'good hands'.

Spring arrived again. The snow down in the valley had not disappeared yet, and the cold winter shadows were still creeping up between the tall buildings, which had been built very closely together. On the sun terrace of Soglio, however, the meadows were free of snow and the alleyways were dry. Houses and stables looked cosy as they were warmed in the spring sunshine. Here and there, the first signs of green dared to show. Flowers, such as crocuses — which resembled little white candles — emerged, and there were coltsfoot flowers with their sun-like faces, as well as the blue stars of spring gentians. Honey and bumblebees were humming around the willow catkins, and on the bare trees, blackbirds sang their tuneful melodies, which floated into the blue sky.

In the Palazzo, the Signora sat in her armchair next to the window in the sunny room leading out to the village square. Alma attended to her, as she needed more and more care. She had grown thin and frail, and she suffered from painful arthritis. Alma treated her with an ointment made of wild herbs, which she had produced by following her mother's recipe. Caterina had died, and Alma was now in sole charge of all work in the kitchen and house. Lisabetta was a great help, as she did not have to go to school over the summer months. There were not many visitors in the Palazzo anymore, because the Signora needed quiet and care. She was keen to have Alma next to her a lot of the time.

When she had done all her household chores, Alma sat in the Signora's room in the afternoons. Her mistress enquired after the villagers, whether they were well or not — she knew them all personally and was still interested in their welfare. Occasionally, she talked about herself, the travels she had undertaken years ago, about her ancestors and her very large family. Mostly, though, she asked Alma to read to her, as her sight had become poorer as well, and reading exhausted her very much. The Signora had been surprised when she had discovered that Alma enjoyed reading. She allowed her to take the odd volume from the bookshelves to read in her spare time. She now appreciated the fact that her ordinary maid was able to help her pass the time, and Alma was only too happy to do so. Indeed, nothing was too much trouble for her to make the old lady's life easier — such was her deep gratitude and loyalty towards her.

While she worked in the house, Alma was lost in her own thoughts and asked herself time and again, how it could have happened that she was no longer able to talk to Lisabetta, not even about an important matter.

On Good Friday, Lisabetta would be confirmed. She had grown into a tall, slim girl, with regular, perhaps slightly severe, features. She had always been a quiet child, and now she had a calm dignity. At school, the teacher had always been happy with her, and at home she assisted her mother without fuss. Apart from school, she helped with household chores and with spinning jobs, which had contributed considerably towards their livelihood. With that, the duties in the Palazzo, and the occasional nursing tasks, they had sufficient income for both of them, so that Alma had never again been forced to run up a tab with Gaudenzio. Two years ago, she had also inherited a cascina and some chestnut trees from a relative, which were on the terrace near Plaz and which yielded more than she and Lisabetta needed. Gaudenzio in Promontogno took the rest and with this arrangement she had a small credit with him in the autumn, which provided security and the certainty that the times of poverty were behind them.

For weeks, Alma had tried to talk to her daughter about her future, but Lisabetta had always managed to avoid this conversation. She either found an excuse to rush into another room — to check up on the milk, to shut a window, to see who had knocked on the door — or she simply changed the subject. Only on a few occasions did Alma succeed in detaining Lisabetta to talk about job searches. Each time, Lisabetta had declared in a friendly, but firm manner, that she would not remain in the valley, but look for work in the Engadin, more precisely in a hotel. Alma was shocked and protested, 'In a hotel? With people about whom we know nothing? With men? Certainly not, I shall not allow this!'

Lisabetta had retorted that there were hardly any jobs in their valley and that pay was extremely low. In a hotel she would be able to earn more, and she could thus also help her mother. Alma did not wish to hear any of this. She was more than able to cope in their current circumstances and she really did not need more to manage, but no, she did not want to see her daughter in a hotel. Lisabetta had not responded to this.

Alma's final argument, 'What would the people say?' had only received a pitiful smile and the dry remark, 'Since when have you worried about what the people say?'

With that, the mother had to admit defeat.

'Alright then, you go to the Engadin if you have to, but not into a hotel.'

Lisabetta shrugged her shoulders and remained silent. Even so, Alma tried a few more times to influence her. The girl did not answer, was quiet and let her mother talk, and Alma sensed that she would not change her mind — she was, after all, cut from the same cloth.

There were not too many opportunities for conversation, because Alma was very much wrapped up in nursing a patient. She had to manage her schedule very carefully to be able to complete her work in the Palazzo as well. Time, however, was pressing now, as Lisabetta finished school at Easter and after that she must surely stand on her own two feet. It was high time to look for a position, and jobs were thin on the ground. She should certainly not leave the search until the last moment.

These worries depressed Alma, even when she went to Giuliano and his sick wife who had been in bed for weeks with a high temperature; no home remedies had improved her condition. Alma spent the night with her, cooked the meals, managed the household and looked after the three small children. In the afternoon, Giuliano took care of the little ones, so that Alma could work in the Palazzo for a few hours, but when he had to attend to the stables in the evening, he was glad that Alma kept an eye on the household.

One evening, at last, the worst of the illness appeared to be over. Ortensia's temperature had gone down, and for the first time she had eaten a proper meal and looked brighter than she had done for some weeks. The children had been taken to bed and the patient had been made ready for the night; Alma and Giuliano sat in the kitchen.

The worst is behind us, Ortensia is clearly improving', said Alma. 'That is very good, because the

Signora returns soon, and you know that I shall then be needed in the Palazzo.'

'Yes, I know, but what next? Do you think Ortensia will soon be ready to look after the house and children on her own again?'

'She will not be able to manage that so soon — she is still very weak and will have to take it easy for a while.'

Giuliano sighed.

'What should I do? I have to go up to Grevasalvas before too long. There is not much hay left down here, and up there I have enough to last until the animals can go out to pasture.'

Like several other farmers in Soglio, Giuliano owned grassland and pasture in the Engadin and a Maiensäss cabin in Grevasalvas high above Lake Sils. This small summer hamlet, as well as those of Blaunca and Bueira, had for a very long time belonged to families from Soglio. Every spring, the farmers moved up to the Engadin with their families, including the whole household, and the animals were allowed out to graze on the meadows there. The livestock spent high summer even higher up in the mountain pastures, while the nutritious grass around the settlements was harvested. When autumn approached, the women returned to the Val Bregaglia with the children. The fathers stayed in the Maiensäss until the hay had been used up. They kept only a small amount as a reserve, in case they needed it if there was late snow the following spring. When the cattle had been 'fed to bursting' by late autumn,[6] the farmers went back home to the Val Bregaglia, too. At that time, winter had

---

[6] The author uses inverted commas around the word 'ausfüttern' and adds 'as it was called' — clearly not a well-known term, which could be translated as 'stuffed'.

often already begun, and the cows plodded down the Maloja Pass in between high snow walls.

'You certainly cannot leave your wife alone yet. Is there nobody among your relatives who could help?' Alma asked.

Giuliano shook his head, sadly. Then he suddenly asked, 'Lisabetta? Could Lisabetta not come to us? She is, after all, finishing school now. She has learnt everything that needs to be done here from you. Naturally, I shall pay her a salary.'

Lisabetta — sure, why not, really? Why had she not thought of this before?

'I shall ask her. She has to decide. I believe that these matters are up to the young — they have to decide for themselves.'

Giuliano seemed a bit bewildered. He probably thought that when the mother had taken a decision, the children had to obey, even if they were already confirmed, but he was also aware that Alma had different views from most other people in many respects, and therefore he only nodded.

When Alma discussed this proposal with Lisabetta, she was surprised to find that she agreed to take on this task.

'Good, if necessary I shall do this until Ortensia is well enough to get by on her own. After that, however, I am off to the Engadin. And as you have so many misgivings about working in a hotel, I could take a job with a family, if that reassures you. But the Engadin it will be.'

It was July before Ortensia was strong enough to cope without Lisabetta. She had not been idle during that time and had made it known in the grocer's in Promontogno, which was now run by Gaudenzio's son, that she was looking for a job in the Engadin.

Not far from the Palazzo was one of the two big village fountains. With three basins and a roof covered by heavy stone slabs, it was the centre of daily village life. Every morning and evening the farmers used it as a watering place for their cattle and the goats gathered there, when they were driven down into the village from the steep hills after sunset. During the day, there were always women doing their laundry, scrubbing pots, milk churns and pails, rinsing vegetables and attending to many other jobs.

Lisabetta was washing Giuliano's youngest baby's nappies when Alma came round with the message that a gentleman wanted to speak to her.

A well-dressed gentleman, who introduced himself as 'Sar Pol',[7] stood in front of the Palazzo. He told her that he had heard she was looking for a job in the Engadin, explained that he lived in Sils, had a farm there, and was looking for a capable and willing maid to work in the house and in the fields. With that, he looked over Lisabetta from head to toe. The inspection appeared to have been to his satisfaction, as he announced, 'You have been recommended to me and I think you can do the job and will knuckle down. You can therefore start working for me.'

That was how Lisabetta took up her job with Sar Pol's family when they started harvesting hay.

---

[7] 'Sar' is a form of address: 'Mister' in Romansh, used with the first name.

Lisabetta 1831–1913

'I am getting married.'

With these words Lisabetta greeted her mother. It was a sunny Easter Sunday. The sweet smell of the cherry blossoms wafted in through the open window: the tree grew outside near the dry stone wall, which surrounded Alma's small vegetable garden. The birds' chorusing filled the air and the sound of the church bells could be heard rising from the valley below, beyond the Italian border. Lisabetta had visited her mother for Easter every year since she had started working in Sils.

The mother's absolute refusal to let Lisabetta work in a hotel after she had finished school could not stop the girl from fulfilling her desire and moving to the Engadin. True, she had not let herself get a job in a hotel — but went into the service of Sar Pol, who owned an impressive farm.

Sar Pol came from a long-established, wealthy family, who also had property and interests in Italy, which he regularly visited. On the way, he travelled through the Val Bregaglia, where he was well known, as he often took on commissions from the inhabitants of the valley for their relatives and business partners in Italy. This was how he had learnt that a competent and hardworking girl from Soglio was determined to look for a job in the Engadin, and it was now nearly twenty years since he had taken Lisabetta on as a servant in his house.

Alma was not surprised when her daughter stood in the doorway on that Easter morning. Lisabetta's words, however, made her prick up her ears.

'You want to marry — at your age?'

'Yes, this is precisely what I wish to do. And what about my age? Is thirty-four too old for marrying? After all, you were not younger, when you got married.'

'And who is the man you want to marry? Do I know him?'

'No, not yet, but you are about to meet him now. Come', she said, into the dark hall.

A man appeared, who had to stoop under the door frame when he entered. Alma observed, astonished, how he slowly stood up straight. A tree of a man. Never had she seen such a tall person. There he was, an extremely impressive figure, with thick brown hair above the clear, high forehead and a beard which framed the well-cut face. He radiated a particular dignity when he greeted Alma in his pleasant, sonorous Romansh.

'This is Plasch', Lisabetta said, and pointing to Alma, 'My mother.'

Despite her surprise and certain doubts about her daughter's plans, Alma could not fight back a sense of pleasure at the sight of the couple — the magnificent man and, next to him, Lisabetta, who only reached his shoulders, although she was tall, too. She was an imposing figure, also, with her well-proportioned, slightly severe features, which seemed more austere because of the way her hair was parted in the centre. Both had stopped modestly under the door. Alma got up, embraced Lisabetta and shook Plasch's hand, urging him to sit down.

'So you want to marry? How long have you known each other?'

The two of them smiled.

'For nearly twenty years. We started with Sar Pol in the same year.'

Lisabetta with her husband Plasch, who was more than 2 metres tall

'You have known each other that long and have only just now decided to get married?'

'If we had been able to marry earlier, we would have done so, but we did not have enough money, although we saved and saved', Lisabetta said.

'Sure, and now you think you have enough?' Alma asked.

'For the two of us, definitely. I have not yet told you, of course, that Plasch can start a job as a "ruttner"[8] on the Julier Pass. Sar Pol arranged this for him. This is a secure position; Plasch will be paid by the regional government office for construction.'

'You are so lucky. Sar Pol is obviously a good patron.'

The job of a ruttner was not easy, and particularly in the winter it was often dangerous. Alma knew that ruttners were in charge of road maintenance. They had to make sure that the mountain passes could be safely used. For a remote valley like the Engadin, the connection to the outside world was vital, especially for the local economy. On these roads wheat and wine found their way into the villages — cattle, fur, cheese, honey, wax and other products of the barren earth were exported and taken to market on the other side of the mountain passes.

In the summer, ruttners were responsible for the general maintenance of the roads: they had to clear them after thunderstorms and snowfalls, repair and secure embankments, supporting walls and bridges, as well as clean the water troughs for the horses along the route. Before winter started, marker posts had to be put into the ground on both sides of the road to make sure that after snow had fallen,

---

[8] The local term for specialist road workers in the mountains is 'Ruttner', derived from the German word 'Route'.

the route could still be found. Clearing snow was particularly tough in the winter, when it was cold and there were storms and wind, but the road needed to be kept clear whenever possible, so that horse carriages and pack trains could use it.

On mountainsides, where there was a risk of avalanches, they first sent a horse on a long rope across the dangerous part and, only when a track had been laid and nothing had happened, could they begin shovelling the road clear. This type of work, which had to be carried out in any weather at an altitude of over 2000 metres, demanded a great deal of strength, stamina and fitness, but it was much sought after by men who did not, like farmers, have their own land. Not everyone, however, was deemed suitable for this work: the rules stipulated that only 'honourable and respectable men, who met the requirements' could be employed. Alma had heard of this regulation, too, and she was therefore very happy that her future son-in-law had been found worthy of such a task.

'I shall continue to work for Sar Pol and his wife', Lisabetta said, 'and at lunch time I shall, as always, eat with everyone at the table, because Plasch will return from work from the mountain pass at a time when we have already eaten. Then — Duonna Berta, Sar Pol's wife, has promised me — I am allowed to heat Plasch's meal, and we can sit together in the kitchen until it is time for bed.'

'Tell me something about yourself and your people', Alma asked, turning to Plasch.

'I came to Sils more than twenty years ago to work as a farmhand. After a few years I got the job with Sar Pol. I grew up in Tinizong.'

'In the Oberhalbstein? You are a Catholic, then?' Alma interrupted him.

'Yes, I was baptised a Catholic, like everyone in the Gelgia Valley. I cannot go to church in Sils, however, as there is no Catholic church there.'

Alma got up and moved to the stove. As she was expecting Lisabetta, she had prepared lunch the day before; pre-cooked chestnuts with a piece of bacon. Thus, the simple meal only had to be reheated before they could all sit at the table. While Alma stood at the stove, Lisabetta set the table. Alma was astonished to see that she took a white, handwoven cloth, with red carnations embroidered in its corners, out of her bundle. She spread it across the table, then arranged plates, glasses and cutlery in the way it was done in Sar Pol's house when they had visitors.

After that, Lisabetta pulled a side of bacon, which Sar Pol had given her for her mother, out of her bag and, in addition, some soft, dark woollen material.

'This is my present for you', she explained. 'You should have a warm dress made from it.'

Alma took the material into her hand and stroked the fine fabric gently with her fingers. Her eyes lit up with joy at the beautiful gift and she embraced Lisabetta with a warmth that was unusual for both of them. Alma then put a bottle of wine on the table, saying, 'I received this from Arnoldo in Castasegna, when I gave him some arnica schnapps to rub onto his painful limbs. We shall now drink this wine together — it is, after all, Easter Sunday today and therefore a special day, is it not?'

Plasch stood by the window and looked towards the hillsides to the west of the village, which were starting to show the first signs of green. It cannot be easy, he thought to himself, to produce hay from one or two harvests every year on these slopes. They were not only steep, but full of rocks and interspersed with trees. One would have to be really careful with the scythe to avoid damaging it.

When Alma took the pot from the stove and put it on a board in the middle of the table and sat down, Lisabetta and Plasch took their seats, too. They did not talk much during the meal. All three enjoyed the food. For dessert, Alma served coffee and, with it, a small glass of her delicious home-brewed nut liquor for each.

After the dishes had been done, Alma suggested that they take a walk. During the midday silence, they crossed the square in front of the Palazzo and went past the old houses, the big fountain with the three basins and the heavy stone-covered roof, to the sunny meadows east of the village. A narrow path wound its way along the edge of the open country on the side of the valley: a leafy forest seemed to drop off like a precipice towards the valley far below. Down there, leaning towards the steep, tree-covered mountainside, nestled the densely packed houses of Bondo. Alma pointed to the small house in which Lisabetta had been born and to the stately, noble palazzo at the end of the village, which also belonged to the de Salis family. Plasch had discovered the small path north of the plateau, which led through rocks and wild bushes towards the mountains and asked to where it led. Alma explained that those farmers who did not move into the huts in the Engadin lived with their cattle high up in the tiny Maiensäss settlements of Tombal and Planvest during the summer. Plasch asked if he could go up.

'It is quite far all the way up', Alma said, 'but if you want to go some of the way, why not? You can then see almost all the way to the upper end of the valley, from where you have come, and down the valley you will see beyond the border towards Villa di Chiavenna.'

Plasch set out on the path, taking long strides, while the two women sat themselves onto a rock and enjoyed the warm sunshine. At their feet, the first colourful daisies, forget-me-nots and cowslips stood out in the young grass, and butterflies let themselves be carried from flower to flower by the light wind. In the chestnut forest below the plateau, wild cherry trees were in bloom, and the fragrance of daphne wafted up to them. Way below in the depth of the valley, the river was rushing along noisily, swollen after the thaw.

Lisabetta looked sideways at her mother. She had not yet said anything on the subject of her wedding plans and had not even mentioned Plasch — neither in a positive nor in a negative sense. Lisabetta therefore began by asking her a question that had been on her mind for a long time.

'Why have you remained alone? Did you never want to marry again?' she asked.

Alma looked at her daughter confused. She was not used to such questions. They had never talked about personal matters of this kind, and she therefore had to think for a moment about how to respond.

'You were, after all, still young, when your husband died.'

Alma was silent for a while and then said, 'A widow is not exactly what men fight over, let alone one with a child. But there were opportunities. Achille would have liked to take me. '

'What, him? The fat cattle dealer from Chiavenna? That rich show-off?'

'Would you have liked to have him as a father?'

'For heaven's sake, no. He would have disgusted me. Even as a child I loathed this man; it always looked as if he was taking a golden watch chain for a walk on his fat belly, and he touched up the cows on the cattle market. He used to stick half his arm into their insides, under their tails, and immediately afterwards he grabbed a piece of cheese from one of the farmers' stalls and began to eat — horrible, horrible.'

'You see, I surely could not do that to you', Alma laughed, 'nor to myself, by the way. Later on it was Tonino in Stampa, whose wife had died and left him with three small children. He was a good man and he had a good heart. I think we would have had a reasonable life with him, but at that time the Signora was ill — you will remember — and I did not have it in me to abandon her.

Caterina could not be relied on any more at that stage; the Signora really needed me. By taking me on when she did, she saved me from great hardship. You cannot imagine the winter before; you were too young. It still sends shivers down my spine when I think back. How grateful I was when I got the position in the Palazzo, and then the apartment in addition to the job. Could I have left Signora Anna, when she needed me?'

'And later?'

'Oh, Lisabetta, by then I was of an age when one gives up on such ideas. Apart from that, I really did not want to change anything anymore. I was comfortable with the Signora and you, too. My life had its order and still does, as you can see, I am content and do not wish for anything else.'

Lost in her thoughts, Alma watched a brimstone butterfly as it emerged from the calyx of a cinquefoil.

'You have not yet said anything about Plasch and our wedding plans.' Lisabetta interrupted the silence.

'About Plasch? What else can I say other than that I like him? I believe that he is a good man. I think the two of you will manage together, at least that is certainly my heart-felt wish. As far as the wedding goes, I do have some

45

concerns. How will this work? He is a Catholic, we are Protestants. I do not know anyone in the whole valley who has got married in the Catholic tradition — there will be talk, here and also up there, in Sils.'

A sparkle of mischief appeared in Lisabetta's eyes.

'Is that so very bad? You have survived village gossip in the past; do you remember? And I am not worried either. I shall find a way to have a proper marriage ceremony. If necessary, Sar Pol will help; he has promised us.'

'Let us hope for the best', Alma said. 'Come on, let us go home. I have prepared some wool for you to take home with you. And now that you have a strong man, you could also take some chestnuts and a bottle of nut liqueur.'

They walked slowly back towards the village, when Lisabetta suddenly asked, 'Don Gerolamo — what happened to him? Have you never heard from him again?'

'No. He has never been in touch, and I did not want to ask anyone — that could have been misinterpreted. But I do think of him every now and then; he was so kind to the two of us. Whether he is well or whether he is still being persecuted — that is the only thing I would like to know.'

They sat at the table with a cup of milk, when Plasch returned and reported enthusiastically that he had climbed high up and could see far over the valley, all the way into the wild ridges and towers of the Sciora Mountains.

His clear, grey eyes were oddly compelling. Alma felt so drawn to them that she could not stop looking at them, and also his quiet and collected face. She thought to herself that Lisabetta was certainly lucky to have found this man. How could these two people have worked alongside each other for so many years on the same farm and waited for so long to get together properly? She knew, of course, what the arrangements were: the farm girls together in one room and the labourers in a different room, usually in a distant part of the house. It cannot have been easy for either of them.

When she observed Lisabetta now, she seemed to be a different person to her; she always used to be reserved, silent and serious. Now she was cheerful, given to laughter, and quite talkative. She teased Plasch, which he tolerated with a happy chuckle. In all the past years, she had been allowed to extend her visit until Easter Monday, and it was assumed that this would be the case this year, too.

'I shall prepare my room for your fiancé.'

Lisabetta was a bit startled at the mention of the word 'fiancé', and then smiled. She had not properly taken in that she was to be a bride.

'I shall make a bed here for the two of us', Alma continued and pointed to the corner between the entrance and the door to the room.

Lisabetta and Plasch exchanged a glance and nodded.

The couple wanted to have a small, quiet wedding, in the autumn. It must not cost a lot, because the few savings they had should not be wasted.

'And apart from that, it is not the custom to have big celebrations at our age', Lisabetta added, when they talked about their future over dinner.

Sils had changed considerably over the last few years. The number of strangers increased in the summer. What sort of 'strangers', Alma wanted to know, and Lisabetta had to explain that there were people who could live without working, at least during the time they were in Sils. They arrived by mail coach, sometimes also in their own, elegant coaches. There were often whole families, with lots of luggage and they stayed several weeks, in order to enjoy the good air and the beauty of the mountain valley, as they put it. This had become particularly fashionable in St

Moritz, not far from Sils. Visitors drank the water from the mineral spring, bathed in the pool and took walks along the stream — 'with long, bright dresses, embroidered silk sun umbrellas, and enormous hats decorated with whole stuffed birds, just imagine that. In St Moritz they build hotels, big houses with many rooms and, I hear, halls bursting with elegant furniture and paintings. This is where these ladies and gentlemen live, but there are also tourists who like it in Sils. And this is why Sar Pol built an annexe next to the road last summer, with rooms for guests, and a bigger place, which we call the "dining room", and a kitchen with a long iron stove. Sar Lorenz, Pol's son, now lives in this new building with his wife, and their former bedroom above the kitchen is where Plasch and I may live.'

Lisabetta's eyes sparkled when she talked about this.

'They fitted out an apartment in the new part for his son, who used to manage the family business in Italy, and his wife, Duonna Carla, daughter of another emigrant from the Engadin. The young couple, who returned from Italy during the winter, will take over and run the house, now called "Pension Viola", while Sar Pol will devote himself exclusively to the farm.'

Alma asked whether she knew the young masters already, and Lisabetta and Plasch burst out in laughter.

'Of course, we have known Lorenz ever since he was a child. He often played in the kitchen, when I was there, and in the stables, when Plasch was there. He was always a lovely boy, and he is easy to get on with, even now.'

'And how about his wife?'

'Since they were married, she has come to Sils with him every summer — a gracious and loveable woman, perhaps a bit delicate for all the bustle in the house during the summer. But Duonna Berta is also there, when it is busy, and Duonna Carla always says that she relies on me. She will spend time with the summer guests, because they expect personal attention', Lisabetta explained.

Alma wanted to know whether Lisabetta was employed by Pol or Lorenz and what her duties were.

Lisabetta replied, 'I only occasionally work with them on the farm; for example, during the hay harvest. Otherwise my duties are in the pension and particularly in the kitchen. I cook for the guests, but of course the house also has to be kept in order, and the laundry has to be washed and ironed, though there is extra help for this. You know, it is just as it used to be in the Palazzo. The guests are decent people, like those who visited the Signora, and I learnt from that experience what happens in such a house. My masters, and particularly Duonna Carla, are very pleased about that.'

Before Lisabetta and Plasch set off to return to Sils, shortly after midday on Monday, Alma had to promise that she would come to the wedding and stay overnight.

'Duonna Berta told me that she would prepare a room for you. She would like to meet you, too', Lisabetta added with emphasis.

First, Alma reckoned that she could not accept this and, in any case, how could someone of her age make such a long journey.

Plasch laughed and put a coin on the table.

'By mail coach, of course. Here is the money for it.'

Alma found it a bit extravagant that she, a simple, single woman, should undertake an expensive journey with the mail coach, just because of a wedding.

'Precisely because of that', Plasch said. 'My parents are no longer with us, nor is your husband. Lisabetta is an only child, and you are all we both have in terms of close relatives — it would be a sad celebration, if not even you, the mother, were present.'

Alma was touched by these words, and it was thus agreed that she would make her way up to Sils for the marriage.

It was a dull, rainy day in October when Alma took the coach for the Engadin in Promontogno. The wedding was to take place on Saturday and Lisabetta's masters wanted Alma to stay in Sils until Monday. She should, after all, get to know her daughter's new home — where it was and what it looked like.

Alma had never ventured beyond Vicosoprano; this journey was a true adventure for her. She observed, with interest, how the coachman drove the five horses, how he blew his horn on entering the villages, and how the people ran into the village square when the carriage stopped. Three well-dressed gentlemen sat next to her in the compartment. She learnt from their conversation, held in Romansh, that they lived in Italy. Danco, a young farmer, had sat himself next to the coachman in the front. He was on his way to the Maiensäss settlements of Grevasalvas and Blaunca, in order to make the final preparations needed before winter, to make sure they were ready for spring and could be used by men and beasts. Every now and then, he bent down to Alma's little window and drew her attention to various things.

'There, that is the path to the Septimer Pass.'

He pointed to the steep slopes north of the village Casaccia.

'That is the way to the Oberhalbstein, where your son-in-law comes from.'

The news that Alma's daughter was about to marry, and the fact that the groom was from the Oberhalbstein, had quickly spread around the village. Once again, she had caused people to whisper. Alma had not taken any notice — she had learnt from an early age to let gossip pass her by.

Immediately after Casaccia, the horses slowed down, as the road began to climb sharply and became steep and stony. All the passengers were jolted around. Alma, however, barely noticed; she was fascinated by everything she saw. The road wound its way up through the forested hillsides and then suddenly emerged at the top in a wide-open valley. The carriage stopped in front of an inn. The sweaty horses were unhitched and taken to a stable.

'Change of horses', Danco said. 'Come, let us warm up in the tavern.'

Only now did Alma feel the cold. The rain had turned into sleet, and a biting wind was hissing at them from behind the inn at the top of the mountain pass. She was therefore not unwilling to follow Danco into the heated tavern, while thinking to herself how much she would have to spend here. She was the only woman near the counter and that made her feel embarrassed. At the same time, she admired Danco, the young man she had looked after when he was small child and who now moved around and behaved so assuredly — 'almost like a man of the world, nearly like the young Salis gentlemen', she thought. He ordered mulled wine for both of them and the hot drink flowed so pleasantly down her throat that she instantly felt warmed through and through.

'This is how old one has to become before one gets to know the world', she thought to herself.

Later on, when the mail coach stopped in front of the post office in Sils, Lisabetta ran towards it and demonstrated so much genuine joy that Alma was touched. Had her daughter been afraid that her mother would not undertake this journey after all?

Together they walked the few steps to Sar Pol's house, the Pension Viola, where they were cordially welcomed by Duonna Berta and Duonna Carla.

The whole family, along with Plasch and other servants, had dinner at a long table in the big kitchen. Alma gazed in wonder at the large stove, the row of copper pans on a rack, and the kitchen sink — a bowl carved out of a large piece of granite with a pipe above, which ended in a tap that could simply be turned on to release a jet of water into the bowl.

Lisabetta and Alma washed the dishes, while the men returned to the stable once more. Apart from the couple, there were no more guests in the house — the season was over, Lisabetta explained.

Duonna Berta and Duonna Carla joined the couple in the living room, and Alma and her daughter sat at the kitchen table by themselves.

'Now you have to tell me, what will happen tomorrow at your wedding. Will you be married in church?'

'Yes, of course.'

'In the Protestant church?'

'There is no other church', Lisabetta smiled.

'And the vicar will do that?'

'Certainly. You might find this strange, but there is no alternative. We had to register with the vicar; he has the church register, and he then made an announcement in church. We had a long conversation, deliberating whether Plasch would be permitted to enter a Protestant church and even get married in it. As far as Plasch was concerned, he was absolutely certain that he could do so with a clear conscience. He wanted everything to be done in the right way, so that we are properly married. Then we discussed whether it would be necessary for Plasch to convert to our faith. Our vicar thought that, if Plasch stepped into our church to get married, he should be welcome just the way he was. And thus, the matter was settled. Sar Pol and his sister-in-law, Duonna Ursula, will be the witnesses.'

'It was that easy?' Alma wondered.

'Well, when the news first made the rounds that the two of us wanted to get married in the village church, there was talk, as you can well imagine, and I had to listen to a few remarks. I did not pay attention, though — I am, after all, your daughter', Lisabetta said with a smile.

'And apart from that, Sar Pol and the vicar silenced the people who wanted to meddle. Admittedly, it has become known in Plasch's village, too, and in some cases tempers boiled over. At any rate, a vicious letter arrived from one of Plasch's spinster aunts, reproaching him in the nastiest of terms and informing him that she had disinherited him. Not that Plasch knows what he could have inherited.'

'Do you still remember Don Gerolamo?' Alma asked.

'Yes, a bit, but I cannot picture him anymore. After all I was so young then.'

'But you know that he gave me my spinning wheel and the green silk shawl?'

Lisabetta smiled.

'Of course. You have often shown it to me, but you have never worn it.'

'Well, you should wear it, then', and with these words Alma took the little leather pouch Giovanni had made for her out of her bag. 'This is my wedding present for you. Plasch will love seeing you in this.'

Lisabetta opened the case and unfolded the cloth, her eyes lighting up. Just like Alma, in her day, she stroked it with her finger and then placed it on her head. Plasch, who happened to have entered the kitchen at that moment, was beaming.

'That looks fantastic on you. What a beautiful scarf!'

The next morning it was cool, but gloriously bright. The sky stretched like a wide vault over the valley. The mountains were already covered with snow, the larch trees glowed golden all around the sapphire-blue lake and cattle were grazing in the low-lying fields in the valley, which had already been mown.

The church was full, with every last pew occupied, when the couple entered in their Sunday best; the giant of a man and the tall bride with the shimmering green-golden shawl over her thick brown hair. The vicar married Lisabetta and Plasch in a simple ceremony that touched all present. It was as if the wedding of two people of different denominations were a matter of course. Alma was deeply moved — she wished with all her heart that her daughter and son-in-law would have a good and long-lasting union.

Sar Pol's family had prepared a delicious lunch in the guest house and the small wedding party sat together until the evening.

On Monday, Alma took the mail coach again and returned to the Val Bregaglia.

It was a good summer, good for agriculture, with enough rain early on and with sunny days during the hay harvest. For the hotels and small guest houses, and for the private landlords in the vicinity, the season was successful. Increasing numbers of tourists wanted to enjoy the healthy air of the Engadin and the beautiful countryside. In Sils, the local population was able to rent out every single room to strangers, and the season continued for longer than usual, as the weather was mild and clear even in September. In the meadows, hay was harvested for a second time and because it was always a good idea to be prepared for a drastic change in the weather at this time of year, every helping hand was welcome.

Lisabetta was among the helpers, too, even though she was fully occupied in the guesthouse, but she loved the work in the fields and therefore went out with the harvesters in the afternoon when she was free. The last cart load had just been made ready and it was clattering slowly towards the village.

Lisabetta brushed her sweaty forehead with her sleeve and looked over to the Piz Lunghin towards the late afternoon sun. Suddenly she jumped. A thought had crossed her mind. When had she last had her period? It must have been over three months. All of a sudden, she felt hot and cold — she knew with absolute certainty. She was expecting a child. Thoughts rushed into her head. A baby now? At her age? She had not reckoned with this. What was to happen now? Where should she go with a child? And how about her job? She would still need to work, because however much Plasch liked his job as a mountain road worker, the salary was not good and would barely be enough to feed a wife and child. Lisabetta stood in the meadow for a long time, while dark thoughts rushed through her head. Eventually she made her way home slowly with a heavy heart.

What would Plasch say? This was the most depressing thought. She could not sleep. She tossed and turned in bed, with problems and difficulties that were about to confront her filling her head. Then she felt Plasch's hand on her forehead.

'What is wrong? Can you not sleep? Have you got a temperature?'

'No, no, it is fine', but she could not suppress her sobbing.

55

Sils Maria around 1880

Plasch was shocked. He knew, of course, that something was worrying her, and he therefore insisted until she confessed that they were having a child.

A long silence followed. Then Plasch said in his thoughtful way, 'A child; that should surely be a reason to be joyful and not sad.'

This made Lisabetta erupt — all her concerns, her fears for the future poured out of her like a torrent. And finally, 'What will Duonna Carla say? And Sar Lorenz?'

'Leave it to me. I shall talk to Sar Pol. He should be the first to know. He will understand and will certainly not abandon us. And he will also talk to Lorenz and Carla.'

He put his arm around her shoulders and pulled her towards him. Lisabetta snuggled up to him, calmed down, and eventually fell asleep.

'Sar Lorenz said that it was good that the child will be born in winter. By summer you could perhaps help in the guest house again, as the child will, at that age, surely be asleep most of the time. Another worker will be needed in the summer season in any case — an older school girl perhaps. She could, if necessary, also look after the baby occasionally. You really should not worry; Sar Lorenz reassured me that it would all be fine', Plasch said the next evening when they were alone.

That sounded comforting and Lisabetta was relieved, even though she was, of course, aware that a lot would change with the arrival of a baby. The income from her work would continue to be welcome — life was not cheap. Soon her family would consist of three, not just two members. She was torn between looking forward to the baby and material considerations. Not so Plasch. He was beaming, happy and proud to become a father, and he pictured a beautiful future with walks and adventures with a child.

The baby was born on a cold day in March, when the meadows on both sides of the Fex were covered with glistening frost. Despite Lisabetta's age, the birth had been quite normal and Duonna Lucrezia, who assisted the women in the village during birth, only needed to help a bit. All went well; the child appeared to want to come into this world quickly. It was a girl, and very small, 'a bit underweight, admittedly', as Lucrezia declared, only to add at once, 'She will have enough time to grow.'

When she put the child to Lisabetta's breast later on and the tiny creature started to suck vigorously, almost greedily, the milk instantly began to flow, so that Lucrezia could reassure the new mother, 'If she drinks so fast and you have so much milk, your poppet will soon be as big as other children, you will see.'

Plasch, who only saw his child in the evening when he returned from work on the Julier Pass mountain road, was beside himself with joy. When most other men always hoped for a son to be their first born, Plasch explained, he, in contrast, had wished for a girl. Then he deliberated a bit — in an embarrassed and shy way — before he came out with a suggestion, namely that he would like the girl to be christened 'Maria' after his late mother, who had died young, 'if you do not mind', he added.

'No I certainly do not mind. I like the name Maria.'

Sar Pol and his wife had already come by in the afternoon, to check up on mother and child, and after dinner Lorenz and Carla visited, too. Their congratulations sounded sincere, although Lisabetta detected a quiet pain, because her masters had already been married for more than five years and were still anxiously waiting for a child. Duonna Carla stood beside Lisabetta's bed and looked down onto the newborn. Her eyes were full of silent grief, as she softly stroked the child's small hands. At that, the baby opened its little fist and grabbed her finger, holding it tight. Carla's lips trembled, and Lorenz turned towards her quickly, putting his hand on her shoulder in a consoling way. They exchanged a long look and a shy smile appeared on Carla's face. They left the room leaning on each other.

Maria was an unproblematic infant. As soon as she had drunk her fill, she immediately went back to sleep, and then she was quiet until she felt hungry or thirsty again. Plasch had made a cradle, which stood next to their bed in their small room at night. It was moved around and put wherever Lisabetta happened to be working during the day. Duonna Carla often occupied herself with the little girl, when she was awake. She had clearly taken her to her heart and would quietly observe her for long periods.

Easter approached and Lisabetta was spring cleaning in preparation for the holidays. Duonna Carla had taken the cradle into her living room to make sure that Maria was not in a cold draught, as she put it. When Lisabetta wanted to pick up her little one, Carla stood next to the cradle and sang the baby a lullaby. Lisabetta stopped still under the door and looked on surprised, noticing a glint in Carla's eyes.

Carla burst out, as if in jubilation, 'I shall have a baby, too. On the day of Maria's birth, when we were in your place in the evening, I was so sad, but then I was so happy with Lorenz, and then it happened.'

Lisabetta was overcome with joy, and she opened her arms spontaneously and embraced Carla, who was but two steps away. Lisabetta only realised afterwards how unusual such familiarity was between her and her mistress.

In December, Duonna Carla gave birth to a girl, who was christened Annetta, and the two girls would become inseparable friends despite the difference in class.

Three years later, Lisabetta noticed that she was pregnant again. Again, she was very shocked and saw nothing but black clouds on the horizon. She could not look forward to the child, although Plasch and their masters tried their best to cheer her up. But she thought of their small room where there was barely enough space for the cradle. Nor could she conceal her misgivings about looking after two children while she was working. And she would be proved right.

Gianin was a lively little boy, who even as an infant took far more of his mother's attention than Maria had at the same age. At night, he lay in bed next to his mother, but he was restless, pushed the blanket away and he drummed his tiny little feet against his mother's body. During the day, he lay awake, wanting company and screamed when he was left alone. Maria did play with him, but he always demanded his mother. He began to crawl at an early age and soon toddled around on his wobbly legs. This brought chaos into Lisabetta's daily routine and she was frequently at her wits' end because of the mayhem he caused; as a result, she often felt exhausted. During long conversations with Plasch, she tried to come up with solutions, but now more than ever she feared that they might not have enough money and be forced into debt. That thought truly terrified her.

Since the wedding, Plasch had started to attend the service in the church where the rest of the villagers went, and it bothered neither him nor the congregation that the man from the Oberhalbstein now regularly came to listen to the Protestant sermon. After church, the men tended to stand together for a while and chat about the prospect for the harvest, the livestock market and hunting. When Sar Pol made his way home, Plasch normally followed him. There was usually not much talk — they walked side by side in silence, deep in thought.

In late summer, it so happened that a younger, well-dressed woman approached Sar Pol and introduced herself as Silvana, daughter of the erstwhile miller.

'Oh, it is you, I would not have recognised you! How are you? You live in St Moritz, do you not? Have you got family?'

'Yes, I am married to a man from Zernez, who works as a general clerk of works in the Hotel Kulm. I wanted to tell you that I would like to have my old mother live with us now.'

Silvana's parents had lived in the mill, which belonged to the village council, where the community oven was also located. The father worked the mill, while the mother had the position of village baker.

Unlike regions where the forests grow faster and did not need as much protection in the higher parts, such as the Upper Engadin, even the wealthier farmers did not own an oven built onto their houses. There was only a village oven controlled by the local council that was usually operated by a woman, the baker or, in Romansh, the 'furnera'. She had to observe strict regulations. Bread could only be baked on certain days. Then, the baker had to fire up the oven and keep it going day and night until every household in the village had their bread baked. Taking turns according to an agreed order, the women had to bring the loaves they had prepared to the oven to have them baked. This was done out of 'consideration for the wood', as the by-laws expressly stated, to use up as little wood as possible.

Since the earliest settlements, people in these mountainous regions had known only too well how important it was to maintain the forests as protection against avalanches and mudslides. The furnera was responsible for the maintenance of the oven and observance of the regulations, and she received a small fee from the community for this service. On top of that, a small 'baking salary' was added — a fee that was charged for each piece baked.

The mill was next to a stream, not far above the village. Since the miller had died it had not been in use — the people went to Silvaplana with the cereal they wanted milled. The widow had continued to live in the mill, and the duties of the furnera guaranteed a meagre income. She was, however, getting noticeably older and sometimes the baking was not as good as it used to be. In any case, she was becoming too weak for the job.

'I am well aware that the women complain', Silvana said. 'The crust is often black and inedible — they reported this all the way to St Moritz, but what can be done, given that her eyesight is failing?'

Sar Pol nodded and said, 'These were only exceptions, and this was not really serious, but I also think that Mother Uorschla, who has worked so hard all her life, now deserves a few quieter years. Hauling heavy pieces of wood for the oven and particularly the long nights during the baking periods are really too exhausting for a woman of her age. I shall talk to the other men on the committee and start looking for a successor to Uorschla.'

Silvana said goodbye, obviously relieved.

Walking on, Plasch suddenly stopped, clearing his throat. He stuttered slightly, as he began to talk.

'I do not know...but I have had a thought now...because of the mill...'

'That is precisely what I wanted to say, too', Sar Pol interrupted him. 'How would it be if Lisabetta took on the work of the furnera? She knows the situation up there, as she often helped Uorschla. I am well aware that you, too, have often prepared the wood for the furnera. This job would really suit you. You could live there, although it is rather small and cramped, but there is a little more space available, and you will need that, as you cannot go on like this for long, as the children grow bigger.'

Plasch's face lit up.

'That would be wonderful. Yes, Lisabetta will be a success. I am sure the women will be satisfied with her. And as far as space is concerned, we do not need a lot, but there is a little lounge and two small bedrooms — it would be marvellous. And your grandchildren' (Annetta had had a little brother two years after her arrival) 'could always come to us and be with our children, just as they currently do, and that way they would not be a hindrance in the hotel.'

Sar Pol smiled.

'Yes, you can be sure they will often be with you, just as they are now. And it is not a bad solution for all of us, particularly during the season.'

Shortly afterwards, the village council elected Lisabetta to the post of furnera, and the family moved into the mill. These were to be the happiest years of Lisabetta's life, even though it meant continuing to work very hard and saving as much as possible, because she was aware that the income from the baking fees would barely add up to the wage Duonna Carla had paid her for her help in the guest house. What is more, she was used to getting extra money through tips from guests, who liked to show their appreciation of the hardworking and helpful young woman with her good manners. This additional income would now be lost. Her small savings had been mostly used up as they had to purchase new furnishings and equipment for their new home. The previous house, which they had rented from their master's family, had been furnished, but now they needed beds and linen, kitchen equipment, crockery, laundry and other household items.

On the other hand, they now lived in their own home and were free to do as they pleased. The baking days, however, had to be observed meticulously, but apart from that, Lisabetta could organise her days just as she wanted to, something she had not been able to do until now.

The mill was a narrow high building, which the farmers could approach from the mountainside in order to empty their bags of cereal into the funnels of the grinder.

One storey below, on the ground floor, they then took delivery of the ready ground flour and could load it directly onto their vehicles. The kitchen was also on this level of the building and it could be entered from the access road. A long table in the front part of the room was ready for the women to leave their loaves. From there, they would be pushed into the large community oven, which was built into the wall next to the stove. Right next to the kitchen, there was a tiny little lounge. From here, a narrow, steep staircase led into the bedroom above, which could just about accommodate four beds. In the small lounge, there was a bay window, which had a view of the village and the mountains on the other side of the valley, and a cosy wood-burning tiled stove with a bench.

On baking days, the whole house was pleasantly warm, but when there was no baking, Lisabetta was glad to be able to light the stove, so that Plasch, when he returned from his work in the snow and freezing temperatures, could make himself comfortable on the warm bench. Before too long, Lisabetta managed to organise her time in such a way as to make it possible for her to take on other jobs beside her baking duties, such as mending the guest house laundry, as well as standing in as a hotel assistant, paid by the hour.

The older the children grew, the better they could help with work. Maria had learnt at an early age how to do some household chores and took over many tasks from her mother. Gianin, too, made himself useful by carrying wood from the shed to the kitchen, undertaking small errands and fetching water from the stream to fill the kettle. One of the children's favourite duties was to take the ready baked loaves to the housewives, who preferred to have them delivered rather than climb the steep path to the mill. More often than not, they gave the children some small change, a so-called 'Blutzger',[9] which they then proudly handed over to their mother. Maria, who had reached school age in the meantime, was a good student; she learnt with ease and loved reading, just like her grandmother Alma.

Plasch found great job satisfaction as ruttner. It was, admittedly, hard work that he and one of his colleagues had to do between Silvaplana and the top of the Julier Pass. He left the mill early in the morning, bread and cheese in a rucksack on his back, and went to Silvaplana, where his colleague joined him. Towards lunchtime, they usually arrived at the mountain hut at the top of the pass, where they met the two colleagues who had to maintain the northern side of the pass all the way down to Bivio. Occasionally, there was news from Plasch's native village, Tinizong, but it was usually scant, because he was considered a defector. This, however, did not trouble Plasch, because he was happy with his life in Sils and always looked forward to returning home to his warm living room and his family.

These happy times were to last only a few years.

On a summer's day, with heavy thunderstorms and fierce gales, Plasch returned home from work on the mountain pass late, completely soaked and frozen to the bone. He went to bed without dinner. He was feverish and started to run a high temperature.

Four days later he was dead — pneumonia, the doctor, who Sar Pol had asked to come from Samedan, pronounced.

Alma had come from Soglio for Plasch's funeral in the small cemetery next to the church in Sils Baselgia. Her heart was aching when she looked at Lisabetta, who seemed

---

[9] A 'blutzger' was an old episcopal coin of very little value which was struck in the Grisons. Blutzgers were made of an alloy containing gold or silver with a predominating amount of copper or other base metal.

to have turned into stone, standing with empty, tearless eyes, next to her two children at the grave. Alma realised how much warmth and simple happiness Plasch had given her daughter. Was Lisabetta really destined to share the fate of an early widowhood with her mother?

Lisabetta was forced to work even harder than before. She took on day-labourer jobs on top of all the activities for the Pension Viola and her baking duties.

Around Christmas time, life was particularly demanding, because of the additional, seasonal baking. According to old traditions, every household prepared 'Birnbrot',[10] 'Bütschellas'[11] and all kinds of other sweet cakes and biscuits, which were taken to the mill for baking. Thus, Lisabetta worked nonstop at the oven during this period, as the proficient housewives were bringing her delicacies that they had produced with expensive ingredients, and which must not, under any circumstances, be spoilt during the baking process.

'You have to go to Silvaplana this afternoon to get oil for the lamp', Lisabetta said, when Maria came home from school. The girl's face showed her apprehension.

'But Mamma, it is snowing so hard.'

While she pushed a bundle of thin firewood into the oven, her mother replied, 'I have run out of oil, and I cannot work without light. Fetch me a small tray from outside, with about five loaves of bread; they should just about fit.'

---

[10] 'Birnbrot', literally 'pear bread', is a traditional pastry originating in Switzerland, filled with dried pears, nuts, raisins, and other dried fruit, such as apples. It also contains candied fruit, coriander, cinnamon, star anise and clove, and sometimes alcohol.
[11] 'Bütschellas' are raisin buns which were traditionally made with water and resemble brioches.

Maria went out into the cold landing. Everywhere, there were trays with pastries waiting to be baked. She lifted one of the trays with Birnbrot and carried it to the kitchen. Since her father's death, even families who had one of the new iron cookers with a baking oven not only brought their bread to the village oven, but also the traditional baked goods for Advent and Christmas. This way they could create a small additional income for the widow. Even so, her mother was weighed down desperately by serious worries, as Maria knew only too well.

It hurt her to think of her father; his memory felt like a burn deep inside her. She saw him in front of her again, this strong man, bigger than all other men in the village; she saw his clear, kind eyes, his measured gait, heard his deep voice and remembered that he had sung for her and Gianin — she could still hear the full, beautiful sound even now.

The mill in Sils Maria around 1860

67

'I shall have to bake all through the night, otherwise I will not be able to finish', her mother sighed, 'and I need the money so much. This is why I need light.'

When Maria wrapped herself in the woollen shawl after lunch, Gianin came and begged to be allowed to go, too. Maria hesitated, but their mother reckoned it would be better for them to go together. Apart from that, Gianin would be in the way of her work in the house. Thus, the two children went on their way — Maria with the empty jug in her hand.

The snow fell in thick flakes. No sooner had they reached the path linking Sils Maria and the country road to the left of the Inn, and crossed the open fields, than they felt the wind coming up and sweeping over the plain, covering the route with snow drifts. Wading through them was arduous, but Maria walked as fast as she could, still allowing Gianin's short legs to keep up, of course. She knew full well that the return journey would be even harder. When they arrived at the main road, it was a bit better, because there was a tailwind. Moreover, vehicles had passed there, and it was easier to walk in their tracks.

The two children trudged bravely towards Silvaplana, though Gianin asked several times whether they had far to go. Maria was glad that the grocery shop in Silvaplana was in the first house at the entrance to the village. With the ringing of the doorbell, Duonna Clelia appeared and threw her hands up in a horrified gesture.

'My God, you have come down from Sils in this weather! What on earth do you need that could not wait?'

'Half a litre of oil for the lamp.'

'What? You have to come such a long way for just half a litre of oil?'

'Mamma does not have enough money for more oil', Maria shyly muttered, 'and she has to bake, also at night...'

'I know, I know. Now you come into the lounge and have a warm drink', Duonna Clelia ordered.

Gianin's eyes turned into big round circles as he admired the mirror with the golden frame, the green plush armchairs and the gathered lace curtains in the lounge of the grocer's house. But when Duonna Clelia put a cup of hot chocolate and a 'biscutin'[12] in front of him, he forgot everything else and happily lost himself in the bliss of such unfamiliar delicacies. In the meantime, Duonna Clelia filled the oil canister in the shop — a whole litre — topped up the children's hot chocolate and lamented that just now no horse and cart, which could have given the children a lift, was passing. She even considered keeping the children with her overnight, but Maria protested firmly. Their mother would worry and, besides, she urgently needed the oil.

Maria and Gianin were then sent on their way with words of admonishment ringing in their ears. The wind had grown stronger and howled in the rocks above the road.

They had not got far when Gianin began to complain. There was a lot of snow on the road, walking was extremely laborious, and the snow was up to the children's knees — so short were their legs. When they arrived exhausted at the upper end of Lake Silvaplana and stepped onto the open plain, the snowstorm hit them with its full force. The road was covered in parts by drifting snow and the children fought an arduous battle against the wind. Gianin started to cry; he wanted to stop. Maria almost had to use force and pull him behind her. The plain seemed infinite. The cold crept into their clothes and they only made very slow progress. Dusk

---

[12] A 'Biscutin' is a typical biscuit from the alpine region of Valchiavenna in the Italian province of Sondrio in Lombardy.

closed in. Maria felt her strength draining when they reached the turn off to Sils. The wind was even worse there. The path was under a deep cover of drifting snow, so that Maria was not sure if she was going in the right direction. Gianin sat down and declared, crying, that he could not go any further. Maria pleaded, scolded, cajoled.

'Let me sleep, only for a little while', Gianin whined.

Maria knew, however, that this could result in his death, and so she heaved him onto her shoulders, kept hold of him with one hand and carried the oil canister in the other. She was out of breath, but battled on. Deeper and deeper she sank into the snow drifts. She felt increasingly tired; her heart beat so hard that her throat hurt. She stumbled, got up again, and struggled on against the biting wind, which lashed, like needles, against her face. With ever more snow, Maria only saw white and did not know where she was anymore, and then she was aware of nothing at all.

At some stage she thought she heard the tinkling of a bell in the distance and her name being called. She answered in a weak voice. The shouting approached and then she felt herself being lifted up by strong hands and wrapped in blankets.

Only when Maria was back in the warm kitchen did she regain consciousness properly, while her mother took her wet, frozen clothes off and dressed her in dry ones. Then she sat at the table, a mug of hot milk with honey in front of her. Lisabetta sat next to her and gave spoonfuls of milk to Gianin, who was still dazed.

Sar Pol was standing in the doorway. Exhausted as she was, Maria overheard — half asleep — the conversation between him and her mother.

'Are you not aware, Lisabetta, that the children would have frozen to death if I had not found them? I would not even have looked for them if Annetta had not implored me — she said that she and Maria had agreed to do their homework together, but Maria had not returned from Silvaplana. I can tell you that it was hard enough to get through with a horse-drawn sledge — how could two children have managed? It was totally impossible to see anything in this blizzard. Fortunately, Maria had somehow had the strength to answer when I called, otherwise I would have driven past them — they were lying a bit away from the path and were completely covered in snow.'

'I desperately needed the oil. I cannot bake through the night without light. And you know that I could not go to Silvaplana myself, either, as I have to stay with the oven. And all of this' — Lisabetta pointed to the baked goods, which were everywhere — 'has to be finished, otherwise I do not get my baking fee. Besides, I have to buy bare necessities for the family. And finally, should I sit in the dark with the children on Christmas Eve?'

'If this is the way it is, why have you not come to me sooner?'

'I am not a beggar.'

'That I know as well as everyone else here in the village. Everybody knows how hard you work. But you must not be so proud that you risk your children's lives.'

Lisabetta covered her face in exasperation but said nothing.

'It is a mistake to think we have not noticed that you have not been so well after this bad year', Sar Pol continued, 'but now I will ensure that you have more regular work so that you have enough income for yourself and your children. Promise me, though, that you will come to me if you are in difficulty.'

Lisabetta nodded silently.

71

When Maria woke up the following morning, she heard her mother busying herself in the kitchen, as usual. She climbed down what is locally known as the 'Burel', a small, narrow staircase behind the oven, and grabbed the broom to sweep the house entrance clear. When she opened the door, she stood stock-still. There was a big basket, full of little packets and food. On top, there were apples and nuts, and above all that a tall candle. The flame glowed softly and shone onto the silently falling snowflakes, at the same time illuminating the dark hallway with its warm light.

After this, Sar Pol and his family took much more care of Lisabetta and her children. She was given the laundry from the guest house, not only to mend, but also to iron. This was work she could easily do while she monitored the oven. Whenever she could spare some time, she took on further paid work which helped her in the constant struggle to make ends meet.

After Plasch's funeral, Alma had suggested Maria and Gianin could stay with her in Soglio during the school holidays, saying 'so that it is a bit easier for you and, when you do not have to bake, you can earn a bit extra'.

She had thought to herself that, without the children to look after, her daughter could work in the Guest House Viola', in addition to her duties as furnera.

'Work is the best remedy when it comes to coping with grief, dealing with guests and visitors can distract her from her pain', she reflected.

The Signora no longer lived in the Palazzo, but Alma continued to look after it. Only rarely did members of the Salis family occupy it; they usually stayed for just a short while and came with their own servants. The apartment in the big house continued to be Alma's home, in accordance with the Signora's wishes. It was therefore no problem for her to have Maria and Gianin with her for some time, quite apart from the fact that she longed to get to know her grandchildren better.

Lisabetta had hesitated. Her mother was over seventy years old — would it not be too much for her to have both these lively children? And she herself would then be completely alone. On the other hand, she could not conceal the fact that, without the children, she would have more time to pursue paid work.

Alma added, 'I will ask Giuliano to bring the children when he is in Grevasalvas in the summer. Every now and then he has to come to Soglio to check that everything is in order here, too. He can then give them a lift in his horse and cart. Moreover, I would like to have the children with me for once. After all, I do not ever see them; should they not be allowed to spend time with their grandmother?'

There was nothing to be said against this argument and Lisabetta could not but agree to let them go. It became clear to her how cleverly her mother had planned this and, in the spring, she wrote to Soglio to say how much she would like the children to travel with Giuliano at the next opportunity.

On a mild early summer's day, Giuliano fetched Maria and Gianin in his cart. The two sat shyly behind him on the wagon, which clattered along Lake Sils, where the fishermen in their triangular boats threw their nets into the clear water. On the mountainside of the road, alpine roses covered the banks. They stood in full bloom and immersed the hillsides in a bright red gleam all the way up as far as the eye could see. Gianin and Maria were somewhat anxious about staying with their grandmother whom they had only met once, at their father's funeral. It did not take long, however, for them to be captivated by all the new things they

73

saw: the road wound its way downhill through tight bends after they had passed the houses in Maloja, down into a valley, where the mountains closed in and rose steeply, jabbing the sky with their peaks and ridges. They were not used to the tall dark fir trees either, nor the deciduous trees, or the bright, unfamiliar flowers in the ornately arranged gardens that they passed. They went through several villages, and then the route climbed sharply on the right-hand side of the valley until, at last, Soglio, the village with its huge chestnut trees that their mother had talked about so often, could be spotted above the forest.

They immediately felt at home in their grandmother's tall, old house. She was affectionate and patient and allowed them a lot of freedom. When the weather was nice, they were taken along to the farms where Alma, despite her advanced age, was still looking after their children and cooking meals so that the adults could work in the fields undisturbed. Gianin and Maria were allowed to play with the children and were soon friends with all the youngsters in the village.

Alma borrowed a smaller spinning wheel and taught Maria the art of spinning. When it was raining, they sat peacefully in the lounge with their spinning wheels and Alma told stories about her youth and her husband Giovanni.

'Your grandfather, who died many years ago. Your mother was very small then.'

She talked about the evil years of the war, brought about by a powerful emperor from France, involving so many countries, including Switzerland, and the Val Bregaglia and the Engadin, too. She also told them how they had had to escape to the Maiensäss settlements in the winter and that this had meant suffering horrible hunger and freezing cold.

Then the children were allowed to look at the Palazzo again: a different Signora lived there for a few weeks during that summer. She, too, was beautiful and friendly, and she showed the two of them her garden. They were astonished by the gigantic redwood trees and the peony bushes whose rose-coloured flowers emitted a sweet fragrance. Thus, a summer passed by that Maria and Gianin would always remember and which, to their great joy, was repeated the following year.

In the winter, between these happy summer months in Soglio, Gianin, too, started school. The lively little boy did not find it easy to sit still on the hard school benches — and he could barely wait for the lessons to end, when he could romp around outside with the other youngsters.

Maria, on the other hand, helped her mother when she was free. Lisabetta took care that there was enough time for homework — good marks were important for her future career. She did not, however, need to worry, because Maria was happy when she could sit in school and listen to the teacher. He let her have a book every now and then. Whenever she could steal a moment, she read excitedly, about distant countries and foreign people, such as the ones she came across in Sils. For example, there was the sinister-looking man with the black cape, the massive moustache and the bushy eyebrows, who looked piercingly at other people, without actually seeing anyone properly — this at least was the impression the village children had.

'He is a poet and a philosopher', the teacher said, and admonished the children for making fun of Herr Nietzsche.

'What does a philosopher do?' Annetta had asked.

'He thinks', the teacher answered.

'Everybody does that, surely', Maria had declared.

The teacher had not been able to suppress a smile, when he explained, 'Yes, I agree, but he thinks about very exalted matters, issues which we would not understand. And then he makes notes about them.'

The children were impressed. Writing, completely voluntarily, without being asked to do so by the teacher or the parents, was a rare occurrence in the classroom. From then on they looked at the odd man with a kind of curious respect.

Shortly before her 80th birthday, Alma fell ill. Lisabetta was informed by Giuliano that things were not well with her mother and advised her to visit as soon as possible.

Lisabetta showed the letter to Sar Pol who declared at once, 'Do not waste any time, go to the Val Bregaglia tomorrow. We shall take care of the children and look after the village oven, so that you can be with your mother with a clear conscience, for as long as she needs you.'

The following day, Lisabetta took the first post carriage to Promontogno to walk up to Soglio from there. The frosty winter shadow was lying over the villages in the valley, while up in Soglio a bright sun shone on the walls of the old houses.

Lisabetta was shocked when she entered her mother's apartment. The patient was so thin, her features sunken and she appeared weak and tired. She smiled, though, when she saw her daughter and said, 'How good that you have come. Now I can die in peace.'

When Lisabetta wanted to object, she fended her off with a movement of her hand and said in a quiet, but decisive voice, 'My time has come. I am ready.'

Lisabetta tried to help with her mother's own, tried and tested old remedies, but she recognised that Alma was already on her way into the next world. Only two days later, as she sat at her mother's bedside, her weakened hand in hers, Alma's tired heart stopped beating.

After the funeral, Lisabetta cleared the apartment. She gave the few pieces of furniture to relatives and neighbours and only kept a few items for herself, among them Don Gerolamo's spinning wheel. She passed them to Giuliano to store until he could bring them to Sils in the spring.

Time passed, and Maria finished her eighth year at school. Her teacher was sorry to see her leave, because this clever and bright child had given him joy through the years, and he had helped her as much as he could.

In the first summer after the end of school, Maria still worked in the guest house. Her friend Annetta had been sent to a girls' boarding school in French Switzerland and Maria missed her a lot.

As the guest house remained closed in the winter, Maria started a job in the Hotel Wilder Mann[13] in Silvaplana; the landlord was related to Sar Pol, and they already knew each other. The landlady, Duonna Anna-Barbla, was an extremely capable woman, who enforced strict rules in her house, but she was also just and gave praise where it was due. On the other hand, she reprimanded her staff strongly when she deemed it necessary.

Maria settled down very quickly, not least because the daughter of the house, Victoria, 'Vicky' as they called her, was the same age. Vicky worked in the house, too, and was treated exactly as her colleagues. She was vivacious and bubbly and always had funny ideas. She approached everyone with openness and was therefore very popular with

---

[13] 'Wilder Mann' means 'wild man', not an unusual name for an inn.

the guests. The two girls understood each other at once, loved working together and were soon true friends.

The Wilder Mann was the stop for the mail coach. When the carriages came down from the Julier Pass, the postilions used to blow their horns just before they reached the big bend in the road above the village. That was the signal to get on with the final preparations for the arrival of the hungry and thirsty travellers. The tables, already laid, were inspected to ensure that nothing was amiss, Maria had to run out to the village fountain and fill all the jugs on the tables with fresh water. In the kitchen, the fire was rekindled, and the 'Gerstensuppe'[14] was bubbling in big pots.

Tired and, in the winter, frozen through and through, the travellers dismounted and first asked for mulled wine, which was served steaming hot. Then they ordered food, and with speed being of the essence, everyone called Maria and Vicky, who ran from the dining room to the kitchen and back. There was not much time; the postilion urged everyone on, because he had to keep to the timetable. Outside, the horses stamped their feet. There were always some people who found the interruption inconvenient and nervously stood by the door, waiting to depart again.

The evening post was more leisurely, because some of the passengers always stayed overnight in the hotel. This meant that there was time for a substantial meal. Duonna Anna-Barbla's culinary skills were much appreciated — she was, indeed, a particularly good cook. The wine from the Valtellina was even more heartily consumed: the landlord had bought it from a personal friend who was an expert winemaker. The hotel was famous for its good wine list. There was quickly a cheerful, loud atmosphere. Chasper, the

---

[14] 'Gerstensuppe', barley soup with vegetables and smoked meat, is still one of the most popular regional dishes.

road worker of the village, who sat in the pub every night with his 'quintin'[15] of red, fetched the accordion from his home next to the hotel and started to strike up. Singing began, there was much laughter, and many tales about the hunt with all its dramatic events were recounted.

That was the moment when Vicky and Maria winked at each other and feigned tiredness to be allowed to withdraw to bed as soon as possible. They climbed the stairs, but not into their rooms. There was a small hall above the saloon where meetings were held, weddings were celebrated and where wakes took place. Without turning on the lights, the two girls slipped out of their shoes, so that their steps were inaudible and danced in their stockings to Chasper's music, which could be heard from downstairs, until late into the night.

Although they had to get up early in the morning and often work late in the evening, Maria liked being in the Hotel Wilder Mann. She earned more than she had expected, and she was happy to be able to give her mother some of it. Lisabetta was, however, unwavering in her refusal to touch that money.

'I do not need it. I am still able to take care of myself and Gianin. The income I get as the furnera is not quite enough, though, but with the salary that I receive additionally from the hours I work in the guest house, we have enough for the two of us. When I have to mind the oven and, quite often at other times when I am not actively busy, I like sitting at the spinning wheel, which I have inherited from my mother — you know, Don Gerolamo's wheel. With that it is easier for me to spin than with Uorschla's old spinning wheel that was left in the mill. The women in Sils

---

[15] A measure, i.e. one-fifth of a litre, 2dl.

also like my thread and bring me the wool from their sheep. Keep your savings, I do not need them.'

'Use the money for whatever you want to', Maria said firmly. 'I, at any rate, will not take it away again.'

'Good, then I shall keep it here and put it aside for you.'

Four years later, the time came for Gian, too, to learn a profession. He wanted to go to Italy like many of his friends and become an apprentice with a master confectioner who had emigrated from the Engadin.

The final school year had begun and Lisabetta had asked all her acquaintances whether anyone knew of an apprenticeship vacancy for Gian. In fact, there was surely not a family in the villages of the Upper Engadin without a son, nephew, uncle or at least a friend who was working abroad as a pastry cook. There did not appear to be a position for Gian, however.

Lisabetta started to worry, as time moved on and spring approached. It was important that Gian found work, as he had to learn to stand on his own two feet. Life would then be easier for her, too. Everything was becoming more expensive; only her baking salary remained the same. The local councillors appeared to think that she had no right to a slight increase in her salary for baking. She was not permitted to raise the price herself.

The worst was the thought that Gian had no other option than to go into service as a farmhand and then perhaps wait for a year or longer for an apprenticeship to come up. The émigrés from the Engadin who had established their own businesses preferred, where possible, young apprentices and experienced adolescents who had worked in agriculture for an extended period less suitable for the delicate work in a bakery. The exquisite cake and pastry goods and the decorating with sugar, chocolate and candied fruit called for a particularly nimble and relaxed hand.

Maria had her ear to the ground with guests, carters and postilions, who all came across a great number of people. As Easter approached, one of the postilions drew Maria's attention to a possibility. A young chap from the Münstertal had to leave his job suddenly, because his father had died. His master, a man from the Lower Engadin, was now looking for a replacement. Admittedly, this confectioner did not live in Italy but in France, in Rouen, to be exact.

This was certainly a bit disappointing for Gian, who had hoped to train in one of the Italian towns, where he would have had acquaintances and even friends.

He did not hesitate for a moment, however, and asked Sar Pol to write to Rouen. When a positive answer arrived, he was happy. As delighted as Lisabetta was for her son, her heart was heavy when she thought of his forthcoming departure. Was this fourteen-year-old not too young to go so far away to earn his living? And to undertake such a long journey alone? His future masters — what would they be like? Would they understand this vivacious, sometimes unruly boy?

If only someone had known them, or if it had at least been possible to make some enquiries from other people from the Engadin, but Lisabetta knew hardly anybody from the Lower Engadin. She was thus full of worries and hope at the same time, while Gian, now that it had been decided, waited for the day of his departure with joyful anticipation and curiosity.

When the spring sunshine had melted the snow enough for carriages to make their way over the Julier Pass instead of the sledges, the big day came.

Lisabetta had used her savings to buy Gian a new suit and new shoes. There were just twenty francs left, which she could give him as spending money for the journey.

Gian had turned noticeably quieter over the past few days, and when the time to say goodbye came, he also fought his tears, and had to force himself to look cheerful. A tearful farewell was not a spectacle he wanted to present to his friends.

Just as it had always been, so it was today — the whole village turned out to say goodbye. Men and women stood in front of their houses; people had even come over from Sils Baselgia. Everyone shook his hand, wished him a safe journey and the best of luck for the future.

Some women were crying and had to dry their tears as they all knew that of the many young people like Gian who had to leave their native country, and by no means had all returned. Often the work was too hard, the country, language and climate too different, and homesickness badly tormented them, with the result that quite a few who had emigrated full of hope, died young among strangers.

Lisabetta escorted her son all the way to the bend in the road, where it joined the main road in the valley. There she hugged him one last time before the youngsters of the village took him into their midst. They all accompanied him up to the bridge, and then he continued only with the older boys. Most of them were slightly younger than he was and had one year of school ahead of them. In his age group, there was only Arno, who would help at home over the summer before starting grammar school in Chur in the autumn.

Full of the spirit of adventure, the group walked on, along Lake Silvaplana, which had only recently lost its covering of ice. Wild ducks and coots had interrupted their long journey to the north for a rest on the mirror-like water and dived eagerly for food. On the mountainside, pasque flowers unfurled their bright stars, and between the crags there were the raspberry-coloured garlands and tuffs of the rock primroses. In Silvaplana, they stopped at the Hotel Wilder Mann, in order to say goodbye to Maria. Her heart, too, was heavy at the thought that Gian was now going so far away; such a young and inexperienced boy. Without doubt, he was tall and strong, but he was, in essence, actually still fairly childlike. She had also saved for him and was glad and proud to be able to give him some money.

The boys were singing as they walked up the road over the mountain pass, which started climbing uphill immediately after the village. From every bend in the road above the houses they gave a cheerful 'whoop!' to the houses below.

It was customary to accompany emigrants all the way to the alp, and then it was time to separate, taking leave, perhaps for many years. At that point, Gian was becoming fully aware that he was also saying goodbye to his childhood and that from now on he would have to rely on himself.

He continued to stride ahead bravely and stopped for lunch on the summit, ate his piece of bread and cheese and quenched his thirst in the little mountain lake. He had not walked far downhill on the other side when a horse and cart stopped next to him and the farmer offered him a seat next to him. That was a good omen for the journey to his distant destination.

It was nearly two months before Lisabetta had the first news from her son. He wrote that the journey had gone well, that he had often been able to get a lift on a vehicle and had thus made faster progress than planned, with the result that he had not had to spend all his money. He reported that the master and his wife were both friendly, but that the work was tough — from early morning to late at night. He did not mind this, however, because he saw that he could really learn a lot.

'You should see the cakes and gateaux that are made in our shop! Sometimes many layers, one above the other, and between them are different flavours of sweet cream. On the outside everything is covered with marzipan, like cladding, and beautifully decorated. The "petits fours" — as they are called here — taste wonderful. I share a room with the apprentice who is in his third year, and he is a good mate, but he does not speak Romansh, as he grew up in the Prättigau, where the master's wife comes from. In short, I am well, and I shall write again. Please say hello to everyone in the village, particularly Maria.'

Maria 1867–1957

The 'strangers', as tourists were called, came in increasing numbers to the Engadin, not only people who wanted to become healthier by taking the waters or using the spa, but also those who brought their anaemic daughters so that their cheeks would turn a rosy colour in the mountains. Indeed, people came looking for interesting experiences on mountain walks and hikes and some were even ambitious enough to undertake first ascents to the peaks of the region. They came not only in the summer, but also in the winter, when the roads were covered in snowdrifts and the houses inadequately heated. There were others who ventured out with an easel to do some landscape painting, and one could meet individuals who sat down at a beautiful spot and stayed there for a long while — doing nothing, really.

In the Upper Engadin, hotels were being built almost like palaces and houses with comfortable apartments, which could be rented to guests — particularly in St Moritz, but also in nearby locations. These signs of the times were noticed in the Hotel Wilder Mann in Silvaplana. The house had been enlarged through the addition of extensions. Next to the old pub another dining room had been built and it, too, was full of travellers when the post carriage arrived, as well as being very busy over lunch and in the evening.

Furthermore, the men of the village met up in the old public bar to play cards and to discuss God and the world. The dominant topic of conversation was the newly emerging technology, particularly the trains, which were being built abroad and in the lower part of Switzerland, and which were considered truly marvellous objects.

Another novelty provoked as much interest — electric power. Nobody really knew what this was, except for one chap. This man came from Zuoz, had lived in Italy for a long time and had only recently returned to the Engadin. His name was Padruot. His family was well respected, not least because it had produced generations of professional army officers who went on to serve foreign rulers.

This Padruot appeared to know simply everything about electricity. He informed the other men in the village about it in some detail and repeatedly pointed out that Silvaplana had a real asset in the 'Ova da Güglia',[16] which flowed, carrying plenty of water, down from the Julier Pass. A lot of money could be made from this stream, he predicted. His presentations were usually accompanied by drawings sketched on any odd piece of paper that came to hand.

While he spoke, his eyes followed Maria, who went in and out swiftly and eagerly, serving the guests in both dining rooms. She was tall and slim, had a slender waist, dark hair with a centre parting, and clear, bright eyes. A young girl from the village helped her, because Vicky, with whom she had so much enjoyed working, was now in a boarding school, as was Annetta, to learn how to run a demanding household while leading a sophisticated way of life.

One evening, Padruot came into the pub and triumphantly waved a piece of paper. He proudly allowed it to be passed from hand to hand in the round and wanted Maria to read it too. She was not particularly interested and had no time, as everyone in the room needed serving.

Padruot remained seated until, at the end of the evening when the pub was nearly empty, Maria yielded to

---

[16] The Ova da Güglia is a stream whose name means 'water from the Julier Pass'.

86

his pressure and started reading. At first she understood absolutely nothing.

'Purchase and sale contract', it said, dated 12 May 1886, and then, 'Between a laudable civic community of Silvaplana, with permission of the general meeting of the village council, as seller on the one hand and Messrs Padruot Roedel of Zuoz and Tomaso Picenoni fu Giovanni of Bondo as buyers on the other hand, the following contract has been agreed.

The aforementioned civic community allows the sale of the following: the sawmill, with the ground between the two bodies of water (including the building used as remise for the fire engines), the right to the water in the Julier Valley on the aforementioned ground, as well as the right to channel the water under the wells near the "Era dellas nuorsas".[17] The agreed price comes to a total amount of sFr. 11,000 (that is eleven thousand Swiss Francs), to be paid in three instalments: the first sFr. 4,000, when the contract is signed; the second sFr. 3,000, a year later; and the third and final sFr. 4,000, on 12 May 1888, at an annual interest rate of 4%.'

Only after Maria had read these lines several times, did it dawn on her that this was about a contract with far-reaching consequences and that according to this document the community of Silvaplana was transferring the use of the 'Ova da Güglia'. The enormous amount of sFr. 11,000 and the numerous other obligations listed on the several additional pages made Maria shudder.

'Are they mad? Surely it is not possible to get such a vast quantity of money together.'

---

[17] 'Era dellas nuorsas' means 'area' or 'plot for the sheep'.

Silvaplana in the second half of the nineteenth century

Electricity meant that there was a future for the mountain valleys, Padruot explained, and thus it was possible to earn an unheard-of amount very soon. He painted a colourful picture for her, describing a golden future for Silvaplana and for himself — 'and perhaps also for a dear friend', he added, with a twinkle in his eye.

Maria behaved as if she had not noticed, and quickly carried the empty glasses into the kitchen. What on earth was this Padruot on about? She was, after all, still very young and did no want to think of a relationship. Moreover, he must be much older than she was — that was obvious looking at his nearly bald head.

In the following days, the whole village found out that Padruot, together with the husband of his sister, Tomaso, a man from the Val Bregaglia, had indeed acquired the water rights. This brother-in-law, who could not do any heavy work because of his weak health, would do the administrative tasks, while Padruot would take on the responsibility for the construction side, as well as everything to do with technology. They wanted to start building a power station as soon as possible.

At the pub in the evening, Padruot had a lot to tell the group of regulars, about the water being rerouted and channelled high up at the end of the valley, through the pressure line, which would lead the water into the small engine building — 'at high pressure', as he stressed — and how the water would then propel the turbine and this would, in turn, produce electricity.

'But what is to be done with the electricity?' one of the regulars asked.

Padruot knew the answer to that question, too. Everything that had so far been powered by water, such as the sawmills and other big engines, would in the future be fed by electric current and thus work much better and faster. And, most importantly, 'It is the end of oil lamps and candles. There will be light in all rooms, bright as during the day.'

'And therefore', he added, 'do you not think the hotels in St Moritz will jump at the chance to get hold of electrical power? Have you ever seen the lighting in the Hotel Kulm, which was installed a few years ago? It is so totally different from the smelly and smoky oil lamps. If the spa hotels expect their guests to continue to put up with such outdated junk, they will soon be abandoned.'

The process of planning, surveying, drafting and calculating was lengthy and time-consuming for Padruot. He worked with great enthusiasm and was thus able to convince not only the participants, but also those who were merely outside observers, of the project's magnificent prospects.

After many months of preparation, the start of the construction phase was to be celebrated with a party for the whole village. The men's choir and the brass band had agreed to take part and a dance band had been booked.

It was a Sunday in early summer when the warm sunshine had attracted people from Silvaplana and numerous visitors from the surrounding villages. There was still snow on the mountains, but the valley looked resplendent in its best spring outfit. The delicate young featherlike leaves of the larch trees glimmered bright green. Permeated by cowslips, primroses and mountain snowbells, the meadows presented a bright colourful picture.

In the Hotel Wilder Mann, everyone was partying and in high spirits, and this revelry was matched in the village square where one speaker followed another; some talking about the technical aspects and others highlighting the economic visions — all predicting a great boom. Electricity, this enigmatic and wonderful power, which had entered the valley several years ago, when the hotelier of the Kulm Hotel had built a small power station for his renowned place, was highly praised. The first electric street lamp was a sensation and the people came from afar to admire this technical marvel.

Indeed, Maria remembered well how she had walked with a group of adults and children from Sils to St Moritz on a summer evening. Below the Leaning Tower in St Moritz, they had admired the iron candelabra with the bright white light locked in a round glass ball. Deeply impressed, they had reached home late at night after a very long walk.

The start of the building of the power station was celebrated on the Silvaplana village square until early morning. The dancing made the dresses fly and Maria went there too, once it was quieter in the restaurant. Padruot danced all night, only with her. He was an excellent dancer, full of character and style. Maria, who was mad with dance fever, was only too happy to let herself be twirled about by him. She was not even bothered that he was not as tall as she was. When, at two o'clock in the morning, the orchestra packed their musical instruments, Padruot declared that he would walk her home. She tried to fend him off with the remark that the house next door, where her room was now, was but a few steps away. He insisted, however, to accompany her to the front door. When they got there, he wanted to kiss her, but held back at once when he sensed that she drew back.

'I have to tell you something. I have now achieved what I have wanted for years and you will see that I shall have a great future. All I need now is a home and a family. Could you imagine…?'

It had not escaped Maria's attention that he was plotting something with his compliments and courtesies, but she had not taken it seriously. Now it dawned on her what his aims were. Deeply embarrassed, she stammered, 'I do not know — I have not yet thought about my future and have no plans at the moment. In any case, I still have to earn money, and that means that I have to continue to work.'

'Do you want to turn into an old spinster? There is no great choice around here; eligible bachelors and young men are rare around here, you know that yourself.'

Maria squirmed; she felt so embarrassed.

Padruot was right. There were only few young men living in the villages. They were the sons of farmers who had taken on their father's farm or were expected to do so before too long. In the rough climate of the Engadin valley, the usually small crofts were not enough to support more than one family. As a result, generations of young men had emigrated, and circumstances forced them to continue to do so.

'But I am so young — too young, in fact.'

'You are twenty and have been standing on your own two feet for six years. Others get married at a younger age and know less about life and the world than you do.'

'I really do not know — I have to talk to my mother.'

'I shall come with you when you see her. Then she can meet me at the same time.'

Despite her confusion, it became quite clear to Maria that she did not want this to happen.

'No, this will not work. I first want to speak to my mother alone.'

He opened his mouth, wanted to protest, but then kept quiet. This girl could be very stubborn. He had observed her these past few years often enough when she was working, and he knew that it would have been stupid to insist.

'It is late, I have to go — give me time.' And with that, Maria quickly slipped into the house.

'He is twenty years older than me', Maria said to her mother.

She had asked for a day off, which was granted, as it was still early in the summer season and fairly quiet in the hotel.

'Yes, do go and visit your mother. When we have more business, you will not be able to. And say hello from us', Duonna Anna-Barbla had said.

'Twenty years — I grant you, that is quite an age difference', Lisabetta said, 'but you are not the only one who has married a much older husband. It takes such a long time for our young men to learn a profession abroad and start a career that they cannot usually get married young.'

She sighed and thought of her son, Gian, who was, admittedly, still very young. How long would he have to wait, though, until he could start a family?

'Think of Artur and Clergia, of Cilgia and Linard, and others', said Lisabetta.

'I know.'

Maria pictured these young people who were committed to each other and whose best years went past before they could finally get married.

'He also had other news last night. He could take on the position of verger, which would mean that we could move into the flat on the ground floor of the vicarage. But that will only work if we get married, because someone has to ring the bells at noon and in the evenings, and on Sundays, and he cannot always get away from the building works, so someone else would have to be there to take over when necessary.'

'And that would be you, I assume?'

'Of course. And I would have to keep the church clean, but I would like to do that.'

'This does not sound too bad', Lisabetta said, 'but you have to decide yourself. I cannot advise you — after all, I do not know him.'

'We shall of course come to see you, together, as soon as possible so that you can meet him.'

Maria told her that he came from a good family, had good manners.

'He would never try to pat or pinch me or the other girls in the pub.'

She told her mother that Padruot worked 'like a horse' and that he was currently building the power station, but she assumed that her mother must surely have heard about that.

'Yes, yes, the whole valley talks about it — this work of the devil.'

Maria looked at her mother thoughtfully. What had happened to her, this energetic, independent-thinking woman, to make her start talking of witches, devils and other sinister figures, just like the old people in the Val Bregaglia used to do?

'Rubbish', she had used to say, but such expressions and stories had cropped up in conversations with her for some time now. Was it her age? But Lisabetta was not that old, after all; not even sixty. Was it the fact that she lived all by herself up in the mill?

After Padruot had, at long last, been able to convince Maria, they visited her mother on a Sunday. His endearing nature made it easy for Padruot to gain Lisabetta's trust and friendship, though she interrupted his gushing tales of the power station project in her normal, sober way, with the words: 'Wait until this construction is completed, and then we shall see.'

He had to introduce his future wife to his family in Zuoz, too, and they chose a Sunday when the head of the family spent a day's leave at home. He could immediately be recognised as the professional officer he was: slender and tall, with stern facial features and the curt demeanour of a soldier. He behaved in a very distant manner towards Maria as well as towards his son Padruot.

Maria could not have imagined a greater contrast between her future father-in-law and his wife. She was small, delicate and spontaneous, and wore a black lace bonnet whose starched frill prettily framed her friendly face, leaving her white curls free above her forehead. She had had nine children, all of whom lived abroad, with the exception of Padruot, the one daughter and the youngest son.

She approached Maria with great warmth. This gesture immediately created a good relationship between the two women, which would last for the rest of their lives.

The marriage of Maria and Padruot was celebrated privately in the church of Sils Baselgia on 1 November, with only the witnesses present: Lisabetta, Padruot's brother-in-law Tomaso and his wife Chatrigna.

Just as Lisabetta had predicted, nearly all of the verger's duties fell on Maria's shoulders, and it had already been agreed with Padruot that Maria would be responsible for the cleaning of the church. In addition, he hardly ever had time to ring the bells, because he was on the building site from early morning till late in the evening, and on Sundays he pored over plans and calculations in the construction huts.

Maria understood that he was totally preoccupied by his work and she was aware that there was no alternative in this hectic construction phase. But she gained much satisfaction from her church duties. These were the conditions they had to fulfil to have the ground floor flat of the vicarage at their disposal. It consisted of two small rooms, a living room and the kitchen with an iron stove. There was even a so-called 'water boat',[18] which was much appreciated by Maria, as it provided warm water around the clock. She was also pleased that there were built-in cupboards and shelves, as is normal in the Engadin, which meant that they did not have to buy much furniture.

It was a good feeling to live in her own house, to work on an hourly basis in the Hotel Wilder Mann and look after her own household. At the same time, she was affected by the topic of village gossip: hers was the house where Jürg Jenatsch had been born — his father having been the vicar

---

[18] This is a water container, often with a tap, which looks like a vessel and is attached to old stoves.

of Silvaplana. Jenatsch was a hero who was still, centuries later, very much in the consciousness of the Grisons population, remembered as an unruly, valiant warrior and politician.

Just over a year after the wedding, Maria had her first child, a girl. They had both wanted a girl, and so her arrival brought them great joy. And yet, this was the occasion for their first fight. He wanted to name the child after his grandmother, Rahel, but Maria resisted. She did not know anyone with this name and she imagined that a child with such an unusual name would be the target for mockery at school.

They had words and there were tears, but when Maria could not be persuaded, Padruot said grumpily, 'Alright, in that case it has to be Marianna, like my other grandmother.'

Maria agreed with this, but decided for herself that she would call her little daughter 'Nina', Mariannina — thus Nina.

The construction of the power station was progressing according to plan, but the costs were higher than foreseen. The money began to run out and, worse, nobody could be found who had an interest in buying the electricity. At last, the power station was finished and producing electricity, but there was nobody who wanted it and nobody who could use it, because there were no facilities in the whole village that could run on electric power. Padruot had hoped that the hotels in St Moritz Bad would be among the customers, not least as they invested in the construction, but they were now not prepared to lay power supply lines from Silvaplana to St Moritz.

Given this situation, Padruot decided to electrify the mill in Silvaplana, which increased the costs again, of course. But this, too, came to nothing, because people had got used to buying pre-ground flour. Only very few came with a bag of wheat to have it milled. It was no longer possible to earn money in this business. In the meantime, debts were accumulating. Padruot and Tomaso went to the well-off farmers, the hoteliers and to the banks, one after the other, trying to get credit in order to lay a power supply line to St Moritz, where they could most certainly have sold electricity, but nobody was prepared to put up the money for it. Bankruptcy ensued and at that time, this was a crime. It was only too easy to infer that the two rash entrepreneurs had been reckless with the money entrusted to them, to declare the power station built with these finances a liability, and consider any further credits too risky.

It was late at night. Padruot had only just returned home and stood at the kitchen table, pale and dishevelled.

'I shall not allow myself to be locked up. I would sooner escape.'

The oil lamp flickered when he banged the table with his fist and gasped, 'Have I not slaved away like a mad man? I have given everything away, the money I have earned over many years, what you had put aside and what my family has given me. And now all of this is supposed to be lost? And how can I possibly be a criminal? Tomaso slept while I worked myself to death, otherwise he could surely have tracked down a few people interested in our electric power. And the gentlemen who kept encouraging me to continue with the power station, claiming that they would buy electricity for their hotels in St Moritz — now they abandon me. All while they know well enough that electric power will be the big business of the future. We can see well enough from the Kulm Hotel in St Moritz what can be achieved with it. But no, they drop me now and, on top of that, take me to court. They will not get me — I shall disappear.'

'Where do you want to go, then?' Maria asked quietly.

'Where do you think? To Italy, I imagine. Somehow I shall be able to fend for myself. There is always work in Italy. And my brothers Bernard and Andrea are also there, in case I need help. They will not desert me.'

As things stood, Padruot had not been able to draw a salary for some time, and it had been Maria who kept the household and family going with her small income from her church duties and the temporary job in the Hotel Wilder Mann. Luckily, the chairman of the parish used to pay Maria directly, as he must have been aware that the work for the church rested entirely on her shoulders. In addition, Maria had taken on work on a daily basis, to supplement her income and ensure that the family had enough to live on.

Silvaplana around 1900. The house with the aqueduct first served as the electric power station, later on as the mill

But now — and Padruot did not yet know this — she was carrying another child, and this would diminish the chance of working outside the house in the foreseeable future. She had wanted to tell him for a long time that she was pregnant again, but she hardly saw him anymore and when he came home, he was exhausted, full of worries and also furious. Thus, she had postponed it again and again, waiting for an opportune moment, and now — how could she tell him at this moment? He seemed to be totally out of control.

Suddenly, he stamped his feet and shouted, 'The devil take them, all of them, and the electricity as well and the power station, too, but they shall not get me, not me!'

With this, he ran out of the kitchen.

Maria felt paralysed, could not utter a word. She could not even think any more. She heard Padruot crashing about in the room, flinging the wardrobe and drawers open, and banging doors. Then he stood in front of her, a bundle over his shoulder, hugged her tightly and gasped, 'You will hear from me; I shall write to you. And, as soon as I can, I shall send you money.'

With a jolt he let go of her and was out of the door and had disappeared in the dark.

Maria still stood there, as if spellbound, trying to bring order to her thoughts. But she was not successful. Everything was so confused and mad — this escape, the business failure, the 'bankruptcy'; a horrible word. A word that was destined to stick with her in the future, too — alone as she now was with Nina and soon another child.

'Mamma, Mamma!'

Nina's whiny voice wrenched her from her paralysis, and she dragged herself over to her room. Nina had been woken up by Padruot's banging and sat up in her cot and cried. Maria took the three-year-old in her arms and carried her into her own bed. The child stopped crying at once when her mother lay down with her and immediately went back to sleep. Maria, on the other hand, was awake. Her thoughts were still whirling in her mind like leaves blown around by the wind in autumn, but the little warm body next to her helped her to calm down again and fall asleep.

The village policeman appeared after a few days and wanted to know where Maria's husband was. Maria said she did not know. The policeman looked at her suspiciously and stated, severely, that she should have called the police when her husband disappeared.

'The fact that you did not prevent his escape is called "aiding and abetting" and this is punishable by law.'

'There is no law that commits anyone to surrender close relatives to the police', Maria answered back, 'and we are talking about my husband and the father of my children.'

'Child', clarified the policeman. 'As far as I can see, there is only one.'

'The other one is here', Maria retorted quickly, and laid her hand on her stomach.

At that, the policeman did not say anything else and left.

Seven months later, Rudolf was born. It was a horrendous birth. The baby was very big for a newborn, particularly since his head was too big for Maria's pelvis. The labour lasted for hours and hours. Maria, who had been working hard until the last day, was tired and, with the labour pains returning, wave after wave, all her strength finally left her. There was no midwife to help her, only Marta, who had for years supported the women in Silvaplana in their hour of need. The old woman had already given up her duties as village midwife because of her age and failing eyesight. As no successor could be found, she was still being called out. She was, however, not able to cope with this difficult delivery and was completely at a loss as to what to do to help. She kept throwing her hands up in despair and lamented that nobody else was available. She did, of course, what she could, but it was simply not possible to speed up the birth and bring the child into the world.

When Marta saw that Maria was becoming increasingly weaker and did not have any strength left to push, she ran to the Hotel Wilder Mann in despair and implored them to get a doctor.

News of Maria's desperate plight had spread around the village and Duonna Anna-Barbla did not hesitate to send a farmhand with the horse-drawn sledge to fetch the regional doctor from Samedan.

When Dr Bernhard arrived several hours later, Maria had already given birth to her child with one last desperate effort. Chubby and well looked after by Marta, the baby lay in his little basket. Maria was unconscious. Only with great difficulty did the doctor manage to bring her back to consciousness. Now he was able to properly investigate her actual condition and he realised with horror that the young woman had suffered considerable internal tearing. By the time he succeeded in stitching the birth canal and thus stopping the bleeding, he was himself completely exhausted.

Maria was so weak that, for days, people feared for her life. Lisabetta had been alerted and, after Sar Pol had said that he would look for someone to take care of her baking duties, she came to Sils to look after her daughter. The doctor visited daily in the small carriage, which he drove himself to Silvaplana, in order to check up on Maria. It was weeks before she recovered slowly and started to take an interest in what was going on around her.

The little boy, however, thrived. Lisabetta put him next to his mother, who barely reacted, to make him suckle, and Rudolf sucked contentedly and then fell asleep peacefully.

Maria had not heard from Padruot for a long time, when a letter from his brother Bernard arrived. He wrote that he and his wife had taken in Padruot, because he was suffering from malaria, was very ill and was not expected to be able to work for a long time. Maria was still so frail that, at first, she did not comprehend properly what this meant. Only when her strength slowly returned did it become clear to her that, for some time to come, she could not expect any support from her husband. He had not been able to send anything since his escape. He wrote that he had been searching for work for a while and hoped to find a job and save some money, which he would give to a countryman from the Engadin who was travelling back home. So far, he had obviously not succeeded and now she, too, had not been in a position to work for a long time, and the small sum that had remained from her savings — which had not lasted long — had gone now.

What should she and her children live on in the future? When she had once expressed these sentiments, Lisabetta replied, rather curtly, that she should not worry right now, and added that she had been able to save some money in the last few years. It would be enough for the near future.

As soon as she could, Maria resumed her day jobs. The people in the village knew how much she needed the income and, wherever possible, gave her any work they could find. They did not object if she brought her children along either. Ever more frequently, she was called out to sick people. Just like her grandmother Alma in her day, she had 'good hands', as they put it in the village. She was particularly talented at treating sick children. She quickly gained their trust and they let her look after them. Even if this meant that she was often on night duty, caring for the sick was still less strenuous for Maria in her weakened condition than cleaning and hotel work.

When she had to nurse seriously ill patients, Dr Bernhard was often called in, too. On one occasion, as she accompanied him leaving the house of a patient after the doctor's visit, she said, 'May I ask you something, Doctor?'

'Of course, go ahead', he replied in a friendly way.

'What sort of illness is "malaria"?'

The doctor explained that it was a serious illness, that patients suffered from high temperatures and that they became very weak. The illness came in phases, which kept recurring. There was no complete cure. Dr Bernhard stopped, because he saw that Maria had turned pale.

'Why do you ask?'

Maria burst into tears and reported that her husband had contracted malaria in Italy.

'Where in Italy is he? In the Maremma?' he asked frowning.

When Maria nodded, he added, 'Oh yes, malaria is common there', and then said, glancing at the crying woman, 'That is all we needed, given that you yourself are not completely healthy yet. But do not be downcast. I shall think of you, and I am sure we shall find a solution.'

This did not exactly sound hopeful, and yet Maria felt a little consoled.

At his next visit, Dr Bernhard took Maria aside and said he had to speak to her. Maria thought she knew what the doctor wanted to discuss, as she had so far not been in a position to pay him. When she wanted to apologise, he interrupted her, explaining that he had not written an invoice. He knew her position and said that she should not worry about his bill. He wanted to talk about a totally different matter.

'There is no longer a midwife in any of our communities, and this is an untenable situation.'

Maria replied that he was surely aware that it had not been possible to find a successor for Marta. She had made it known that the fee for being on standby was very low and, in addition, there were so many new regulations about everything a midwife had to carry with her and about her duties, that it would probably be very difficult to find a woman prepared to take on this job.

'No wonder', grunted Dr Bernhard. 'Our canton established regulations for midwives nearly a hundred years ago and at that time they were really ahead of their time; with comprehensive rules about dress code and equipment, as you rightly say, and instructions about lifestyle. Medical instruments were made available and women were prepared for their tasks by senior midwives. Considering the time, this was a great step forward in baby health. Times, however, have changed. Much more is known about births and the treatment of women who have recently given birth and the care of newborns. For this reason, the canton wants to offer a better education for midwives.'

With that, Dr Bernhard produced a piece of paper, which he handed to Maria to read. She gathered from the information that a course for midwives was offered in Chur and lasted six months.

'You will attend this course', Dr Bernhard stated in a curt tone.

'But Doctor, how on earth could I do that? I have two small children, and you know full well that I do not have the money to pay for it.'

'The canton pays a daily allowance; read here', the doctor said and pointed to the final paragraph. 'And, if this is not enough, I shall make sure that the communities contribute something. We cannot go on this way, that is for certain, with all these problem births and nobody who is a real expert, and when it is almost too late they call me to perform miracles and help these poor women. We cannot continue to accept responsibility for this situation; this state of affairs is truly medieval.'

Maria wanted to make further objections, but he dismissed them, arguing, 'You are the right person. I have seen this often enough now. You can deal with patients, you are punctual and reliable, you are steady and stay calm, even when there are accidents and problems and you do not lose your head. And you are also intelligent. I am confident that you will have no difficulties completing this course.' Before Maria could ask anything else, he marched out of the door with long steps and climbed into his horse-drawn carriage.

Dr Bernhard took the matter into his hands at once and sorted everything out. He spoke to Lisabetta and negotiated a financial contribution with the communities, so that the sixty-year-old grandmother was not forced to find another job while she cared for the children and kept house for them. He then enrolled Maria for the course in Chur and could thus present her with a fait accompli.

Maria still had concerns, but on the other hand it was clear to her that this was a unique opportunity for her. Learning had always been something she had been passionate about. How she had envied Annetta and Vicky who had been able to go to boarding schools. Now she, too, had a chance to continue her education and learn a profession. This had always been her wish.

Of course, the problem of childcare for Nina and Rudolf had to be solved. Lisabetta declared that she was ready to give up her post as furnera and to move into the churchwarden's apartment. This way, the children and the church duties were taken care of at the same time.

The training to become a midwife, in Chur, was as demanding as it was interesting for Maria. The long hours alone, never mind sitting at a school desk and listening to doctors and midwives who had been educated in Zurich and St Gallen, seemed hard work for Maria, as she was used to continuous movement and to strenuous manual labour. During the first few days, when the syllabus focused on theory, she could not fully concentrate on the lectures. That soon changed, however, as the material that was taught interested her, and she listened with close attention. There was so much to learn about the female body and its functions, about pregnancy and birth, and also about newborn children and how to look after and feed them. Students on the course had to pay careful attention, memorise a lot and, in addition, take as many notes as possible. The laws and rules which regulated the tasks of the midwives had to be learnt.

Grisons had been progressive when it came to midwifery services and had already organised courses in obstetrics in 1780. Moreover, there had been proper, written regulations in this area since 1808. According to these, midwives were given a small, monthly retainer. In return, they had to be available to attend every woman who called them at any time.   Over the years, the courses were broadened and, in the 1890s, the period of instruction was extended. 'Only the best candidates', according to one of the rules, would be allowed to take the courses. They had to 'lead an honourable, reverent and sober life and they had to be able to read and write well'.

There was indeed a group of Maria's colleagues for whom this clause caused great difficulties, because their German was inadequate, as they came from pure Romansh regions. Maria had the advantage that she had always had to deal with German-speaking guests in the pension in Sils and in the Hotel Wilder Mann, which meant that she could read and write this language.

The linguistic problems meant that it was difficult to motivate women in some valleys to be trained as midwives and this was even more the case because many, particularly those from poorer families, preferred to use unqualified midwives. They cost less or nothing and were satisfied and happy enough to be given a piece of dried meat or some other natural produce. Among these 'wise women' there were, admittedly, some who had a great deal of experience and skill, which suited some communities quite well, as this way they could save the contributions towards the costs of the midwife, which the canton demanded. It had to be said, though, that the pay was low, even for the qualified midwives, both for assisting the birth as well as for post-natal care, which had to be administered for at least eight days after the birth.

There were exact rules governing the dress code of midwives and what instruments and medicines they had to carry with them at all times. In addition, they were not to leave a woman in labour before the afterbirth had been expelled, or when a doctor had to be called. They were also taught how to handle newborns. There was a book entitled *Norms for the sanitary treatment of infants* to which they could refer. The training did not only consist of theoretical subjects; the students were also brought in to observe women in childbirth, so that they could be shown all the practical aspects, including various actions and manipulations with which they had to become familiar.

At the end of the course, the future midwives had to make the following pledge under oath during a festive ceremony: 'We hereby solemnly promise in loyal fulfilment of the midwifery profession entrusted in us to provide all possible help, during day or night time, to poor or wealthy people. We pledge to live a moral life and, in general, display caring behaviour and persevering patience to women in labour. We vow not to contravene the rules of medical practice and to demand and call for a doctor if required. We promise to live according to the instructions outlined in these regulations and to follow all laws and decrees in detail.'

The first birth after Maria had graduated with good marks was to test her abilities as a midwife. Dr Bernhard came past and asked, 'Could you come to St Moritz with me? I have a young woman there who makes everyone nervous with her anxiety and fear. As far as I know, the pregnancy is completely normal, but it is probably her rather older husband who makes her panic. He is so dramatic that he would unsettle any woman, and particularly his very young and inexperienced wife, of course. The couple have recently taken over the parents' hotel in St Moritz and the young woman has so far not had an opportunity to build her own circle of friends and meet other women who could have taken her fears a little. But you, Maria, might possibly be able to succeed; after all, you have a lot of experience with children', he added, a touch maliciously.

St Moritz around 1900

Maria was wide-eyed when she was received by a pageboy in uniform and white gloves at the entrance of the hotel and was then taken along carpeted corridors to the private apartment of the hotelier family. She examined the expectant mother with Dr Bernhard and did not find any cause for concern either. She encouraged the woman as best she could and explained that she would be on standby because the baby was expected in the next few days. Indeed, the woman seemed to be more confident by the time Maria left the hotel with the doctor.

The hotel coach was waiting outside to take Maria back to Silvaplana. She was slightly embarrassed to be driven into Silvaplana in an elegant landau carriage, just like a hotel guest at the spa.

When the horse and carriage stopped in front of the vicarage, Lisabetta appeared at the door and she, too, was wide-eyed. Then she chuckled and said, 'Well, well, what a start!'

A few days later the time had come. Maria was picked up by carriage again and taken to the hotelier's private apartment. She found the woman trembling and sobbing, totally beside herself with anxiety and fear. This was no wonder, admittedly, because the husband constantly charged in and out of the room, gave orders, shouted at the staff and behaved as if he had taken leave of his senses. He wanted the doctor to be present at the birth at any cost, but he was out and about and could not be reached. Maria tried to explain to him that, so far, everything had proceeded normally and that there was no cause for concern.

Labour had started. So far it was only weak, and the pains occurred at long intervals, but that would change.

'What your wife now needs more than anything else is peace and quiet so that she can save her energy for the time when she needs it later on. When that moment comes I shall call you', Maria told the agitated husband, and ushered him politely, but firmly, out of the room.

Only now could she take care of all the preparations needed for the birth. That was, unsurprisingly, not difficult in this well-appointed hotel apartment: there was laundry, good lighting, and also warm water in abundance. Maria sat herself next to the young woman, held her hand and comforted her with encouraging words.

The patient calmed down slowly. Her baby, a small but strong boy, was delivered without any complications only a few hours later.

With this delivery, Maria's reputation in the valley was established.

The happy mother was touchingly grateful and praised the new midwife far and wide.

There had been no birth for Maria in Silvaplana during her first year, but several in St Moritz. With the growth in tourism, new jobs had been created. Young couples had settled there, and they had offspring. That created a reasonable amount of work for Maria in St Moritz and also in Pontresina.

Admittedly, it was quite complicated to get to the expectant mothers in Samedan or Pontresina. Most families could not afford to fetch Maria with a horse and cart, so she had to use the mail coach or walk. This happened very often and in all weathers; in the winter, the roads were covered with snow and it was often bitterly cold. Although every farmer or carter she met on her way gave her a lift, she often had to cover long distances on foot. Naturally, the other houses were not as well furnished and equipped as the Hotel Engadinerhof. Births in badly heated little rooms with only the dim lighting from an oil lamp were the norm. Water had to be heated in the kitchen and, in some cases, carried up a narrow steep staircase to the room above, which was awkward.

For a birth in a wealthy family in Samedan, the expectant woman had already made it plain during the antenatal examinations that Maria would live in a room in their house when the time drew near, and would have to stay until the postnatal care was finished. That was an unusual luxury for Maria. She could, however, accept the offer in good conscience because Lisabetta was in her home. She had given up her position as furnera in Sils and moved into Maria's house where she cared for Nina and Rudolf, kept house and fulfilled all of Maria's church duties when her daughter was absent with her professional obligations.

111

Naturally, Maria made herself useful in the pharmacist's house whenever she could. She would have felt guilty sitting leisurely around enjoying 'time off' once she had finished all midwifery-related tasks, especially since she was paid for the whole day and not only for the few hours that were needed for the care of the mother-to-be.

There was an unpleasant situation at a birth in Celerina. Maria delivered a woman's third child — there were already two girls in the family. After a normal birth, when she handed the mother the newborn to take her into her arms, the first question was, 'What is it?' When Maria told her that it was a girl, the woman sobbed inconsolably.

'My husband so much wanted a son. I do not dare to tell him it is only another girl', she said tearfully, and buried her face in the pillow.

'I shall tell your good husband myself', Maria said resolutely, and this she did.

The man, one of the important gentlemen in the village, uttered a profanity and left the house at once for the pub. Maria decided to stay overnight. She heard him return late at night and, crashing about, looking for the room that had been prepared for him.

The next few days he did not show himself and his wife became ever more depressed. Her husband had not once come to see her. She lay apathetically on her pillows, hardly ate, cried repeatedly and began to run a temperature. Maria was worried and when she heard the father enter the house after several days, she went to him at once and reproached him.

'Your wife cries her eyes out and is getting increasingly weaker from disappointment and grief.'

He blushed and began to curse these womenfolk who can do nothing other than bring more womenfolk into the world. At that, Maria, grabbed him by the lapel and said, 'Women are in no way responsible for the gender of the child, be it a boy or a girl. How can you behave in such an unreasonable way? You want to harvest carrots but have sown cauliflowers and that is how it is. And now you go upstairs to your wife and say something nice and loving to her, otherwise…'

'Otherwise what?' he asked with a sarcastic grin.

'Otherwise the whole village will soon know what sort of husband and father you are.'

It slipped out of Maria's mouth. She then remembered the vow of discretion she had taken at her graduation ceremony. But this gentleman was unlikely to be familiar with that, she thought slyly; his reputation in the village was far more important to him.

Later on, when she was alone with the woman — a gentle and indulgent creature — she said, 'At last, my husband has come to see me. He obviously needed a bit of time to get used to the idea that he now has three girls, but he is still kind and lovable. No doubt this is how it works with men; they need time for something like that.'

'Evidently, yes', Maria quipped, 'and sometimes a prod… I mean encouragement.'

The new mother asked, astonished, what she meant by this.

'Is that not what one says? Maybe he has been pushed somehow and perhaps he has just had second thoughts.'

No harm done if the poor woman really believed that her husband had seen sense all by himself. Most importantly, she was smiling again. Maria asked herself afterwards, though, whether she had been too harsh with the husband. If this important individual wanted to take revenge and pay her back, that could perhaps have unpleasant consequences for her. But then she decided that he would disgrace himself if he made this episode public.

Her job as a midwife gave her great satisfaction, the more so because every birth had gone well. She was well aware that there had been some tricky situations, but she had reacted correctly. All the women she had cared for had been spared from the feared puerperal fever. Maria had, of course, been meticulous with all the necessary precautions, for she had learnt how to prevent her patients from catching this illness.

Even more threatening were heavy haemorrhages after the birth: there was no medication against them, nor were there any precautionary measures. Weaker women were often affected, particularly women who had had several babies, and particularly at risk were those who had had overly short intervals between births. In such cases, Maria found herself forced to have a serious word with the husbands and draw their attention to the danger that their wives were in. Sometimes the spouse reacted by forbidding any 'meddling' and insisted on his rights and needs as a man.

'I am, after all, not made of wood', Maria heard more than once. She did not allow herself to be ruffled, though, and explained sharply that he, like others, had other options — perhaps even with other women? This, however, concerned the mother of his children; did he really want to risk losing her? Such remonstrations did not always make her popular everywhere and she knew well enough that she was a topic of conversation in the pub. She could not care less, of course — this was about the mothers' lives, and she felt strong and secure in her convictions.

It was much more difficult to take such a firm position when women in despair came to her to ask for an abortion. Often she felt great pity for these mothers, who were alone with a whole gaggle of children, because the father, like many others, had to look for work abroad. She also pitied the young ignorant girls who were chatted up by a man and then fell pregnant with an illegitimate child, something considered a terrible disgrace, weighing heavily on the mother and the child. But Maria knew only too well that she must not break the law — if she had done that, her own existence, and that of her mother and her children would have been at risk. However, she never failed to help these mothers, as far as she could, in every other possible way.

She loved her profession, even though the retainer she received as a midwife and the fee per birth and postnatal care were not enough for her and her family, and had to be supplemented by temporary jobs every now and then. Nevertheless, the steady income provided the type of security which made the struggle for survival much easier.

The co-operation of the doctor worked very well and was based on mutual respect and recognition. Fortunately, unusually difficult births occurred only rarely, but Maria always knew in time, thanks to her training and her excellent powers of observation, when the doctor had to be called, and he held her in high regard for that.

Increasingly, he often pointed out, however, that her home in Silvaplana was too far from Samedan and Pontresina, which were also part of her catchment area.

'If a birth occurs prematurely or unexpectedly and a horse and cart have to be sent from Pontresina to Silvaplana to fetch you, you might well arrive too late', Dr Bernhard explained. 'It would be good if you lived more centrally.'

Maria knew well enough that he was right and the thought that she might, indeed, once turn up too late, worried her constantly. It was, of course, the case that Pontresina and

St Moritz had the most births. She had therefore already been looking for a home nearer to her expectant mothers. That proved to be far from easy. The old houses in the Engadin were not constructed in a way that made it possible to separate a part and let it. In newer houses, like those that were being built in St Moritz, the apartments were too expensive.

The husband of a new mother drew her attention to the fact that there was an empty house in Celerina, which could perhaps be rented. It belonged to three old spinsters who lived next door. They were said to be a bit strange and eccentric, but he lived in the neighbourhood and had never noticed that they had ever done anyone harm. Even so, there was talk and various nasty, but untrue, rumours about them circulating in the village. It was even said that they were witches, but he assumed she would not believe such stuff and be frightened. Maria had laughed.

'That is just stupid gossip, to which I do not listen.'

Sar Robert had added, 'The three ladies come from a noble family. They came into possession of the two houses by inheritance and they now live in one of them — totally secluded. They have a few peculiar habits, which may have led to the rumours.'

On the way home from a new mother, Maria did not take the shortest route to Silvaplana, through the forest via St Moritz. Instead, she took the dusty road to Celerina, which led from the hill of San Gian with its church that could be seen from far and wide. Leaning against the wooden railing of the bridge, she looked down into the clear water of the Inn, which was running along with a quiet murmur, making small rippling waves, and leading into a wide loop on the Champagnatscha plain. A few steps from the bridge there was a washhouse by the river. It consisted of only two side walls and a roof. Four women knelt on a raised terrace, busy soaping and scrubbing their laundry against a board, which was leaning towards the water.

One of the women noticed that Maria looked interested and called her, laughing, 'Do feel free to come closer and inspect our washhouse. You will find that it is a particularly good practical facility', and the washer woman started turning a handle. Soon the floor of the washhouse was raised, along with the women. Only now did Maria realise that it was fastened to two spindles at the horizontal side of the hut and that it could thus be adjusted, depending on the water level — a rather convenient invention, given the arduous task of washing, Maria thought.

Celerina – the washhouse at the Inn. In the background to the left: the house whose owner would later be Maria

Maria let them talk, then interrupted the prattle and said, 'Surely that is not so bad; it sounds more like harmless quirks to me.'

On the meadow next to the washhouse the laundresses had spread out the sheets to be bleached, and two children wandered cheerfully from one piece to the next with their watering cans and poured water over them so that the sun could play its part in the bleaching and drying process.

One of the women, rinsing heavy, unwieldy sheets in the river with big arm movements, had clearly heard of Maria, because she asked whether she was the midwife.

When Maria said yes, a conversation began at once. Maria told them why she had come to Celerina that day.

Now there was loud chattering, as if a hawk had descended into a chicken run. All four women talked over each other, making it impossible to understand everything.

Maria did gather from this excited torrent of words that they were talking about the two houses on the other side of the street, which belonged to the three sisters.

'But there is something creepy going on there. They are a bit weird, one only has to see how one of them walks through the village with her umbrella upside down, the tip in her hand and the crook on the ground. And the other one, who always wears an elegant outfit, as if she were an aristocrat, and then there is the third, who hardly ever leaves the house. But they are from a good family, and there is a glass containing a snake on the chest of drawers.'

The women did not accept this; again and again, they talked about witches and warned Maria not to take a rash step. She, however, announced firmly, 'Now I want to meet these three ladies and then we shall see. In any case, I am not frightened of witches.'

She walked with determination towards one of the houses. It was separated from the Inn only by a garden with neat vegetable beds and pretty borders. The house gave a perfectly friendly impression with its south-facing façade, the dark-green shutters, the clear window panes and the polished, shiny brass knocker on the front door, which consisted of a big round gate with a built-in door for everyday use — a typical Engadin door.

In response to her knock, a gaunt person opened the upper part of the smaller door. She was dressed in a simple, dark garment, and wore an apron and a head scarf. She looked quizzically at Maria but did not say a word. Maria explained why she was there. In silence, the woman then opened the lower part of the door, too, walked across the large corridor with its high ceiling towards the closest door and bid Maria enter.

A lady with a broad-rimmed hat of grey velvet, which was attached to her head with two hatpins, each decorated with a pearl, got up from a chair at the round table in the centre of the room. Maria was a bit taken aback by what was a truly elegant outfit. The lilac silk blouse with black lace and the skirt made of delicate, black material looked very ladylike. A big cameo brooch representing the head of a woman was pinned to the banded collar, which reached up to just under her chin. Somewhat confused, Maria explained the reason she had come, upon which the woman introduced herself, saying her name was Giuditta. Referring to her sister who had stayed in the door, she said, 'This is Anna, and over there' — pointing towards one of the windows — 'that is Annetta.'

Only now did Maria notice that a small, delicate little person sat in the red plush armchair and smiled at her in a friendly way.

Giuditta sat down at the table again, on which lay an open book, and explained, 'Actually, we have never considered renting out the house next door.'

Maria described her position in detail, including the need to find an apartment. She spoke frankly about her financial situation, which meant that she could not afford a high rent, but explained her readiness to spend a fair amount.

'Celerina — that would be a particularly convenient location for me and also for expectant and new mothers, right between Pontresina, Samedan and St Moritz.'

While she spoke, she looked around the room. There was, indeed, a glass with a snake in it on a chest of drawers next to the door, between two silver candlesticks. A delicately made display cabinet in the corner contained precious glasses in two colours, beautiful artistically painted porcelain and two silver jugs on a tray.

Under a glass cover on the sideboard, there was a clock whose face was supported by two golden columns with a boy leaning on it at the left and a girl on the right. The activity of the woman by the window, however, fascinated Maria more than any of this: her nimble fingers made the little wooden dowels, hanging from threads, fly backwards and forwards. They were, in turn, attached to a cushion on the small table.

'Have you never seen this? Do you know what it is?' the little lady asked Maria and then said, when Maria shook her head, 'This is called "tatting".[19] Come closer and see how it is done.'

Maria moved closer. She observed, astonished, how these dowels moved with unbelievable speed and how a beautiful strip of white lace emerged. She was almost startled when she heard Giuditta's voice, 'The house has

---

[19] The word in German is 'klöppeln', i.e. lace-making or 'tatting'.

been uninhabited for years and will probably need a lot of work before anyone can live in it again.'

'You do not have to worry about that', Maria reassured her. 'I shall clean and tidy it properly with my mother; she is still very active for her age.'

Giuditta looked at her sisters thoughtfully and asked what their opinion was.

'We shall have to think it over and talk about it. Once we agree, we shall let you know.'

'Maybe she could look at the house now', Anna remarked, standing by the door.

'Ah well, of course, but the house has been empty for so long that the interior will not seem up to much', Giuditta said. 'By all means, though, do have a look. Anna, go there with Duonna Maria.'

Anna took a big, rusty key out of a drawer and went ahead. Maria followed. It took some effort to unlock the day door, as it had not been opened for a long time. There was a dark spacious corridor — its walls and ceiling were covered in grey spiders' webs. Anna tried to open the whole gate, but she did not succeed. The fittings were too rusty.

'It looks as if we will have to find our way in the dark', she said.

Maria's eyes had already got used to the limited light available. The next door led to the living room. Anna pushed the shutters open and Maria looked around. The room was similar to the one in the adjoining house, but of course without the beautiful furniture the sisters owned. The walls were panelled with pine wood and there was a built-in stove in the corner with a wooden trellis on top. Everything was covered in thick dust. Once scrubbed, however, it would certainly make a cosy living room, Maria thought. The kitchen next door was big and gloomy. The only window overlooked the very narrow lane between the two houses, so that not much light could enter. Upstairs there were two bedrooms, which could only be reached via the small staircase behind the stove. The big, northern part of the house was occupied by the stable and the barn. It would take a lot of hard work to clear this house. Maria realised this at once, but felt that she and Lisabetta could definitely manage it. It was, in any case, exactly what she needed. She could only hope that the sisters would let her rent the house.

Back home in Silvaplana Maria told her mother about her conversation with the three women and about viewing the house. Lisabetta thought that it would really be ideal if they could live in Celerina and said that the cleaning and removal work was not going to put her off.

'We are both used to knuckling down.'

They also deliberated over whether they needed the consent of Maria's husband to move. At the moment, however, Maria did not even know where he was. He very rarely wrote, usually only when he had been overcome by his illness. On these occasions he sent short, depressing notes, penned in wobbly handwriting. When he was better, he moved around, looking for work, and often only informed his family of his new address after a long silence. He had only just moved again, and Maria's letters had been returned as undeliverable.

Lisabetta therefore thought, 'We must not lose time looking for Padruot. We have to grab the opportunity, if the sisters agree.'

Indeed, this was what happened. The sisters let the house to Maria for a modest rent. Lisabetta and Maria scrubbed and cleaned for days and when all the rooms were neat, the windows clean and sparkling, the house had a friendly and inviting feeling about it.

In the autumn, just when Nina started primary school, a farmer transported what few household and personal effects they had with his cart from Silvaplana to Celerina. The little family furnished their new home and very quickly settled down. Maria already knew several families from her life as a midwife, and Nina and Rudolf soon made friends with some of the other children in the village.

To start with, they were a bit shy towards the owners, but that, too, passed after a short while, because nothing bore out the predictions of the gossip mongers. Admittedly, the sisters kept a certain distance from Maria and her family, and this was probably how they had been brought up, but they were always friendly. Every now and then they gave the children sweets, which they received from France, and they let them come into their living room, where the children were allowed to marvel at the unusual treasures among the furnishings. Maria and Lisabetta offered to help them, when they needed support, and it was not long before Lisabetta was allowed to lend them a hand with cleaning and gardening — and she was paid for her work. In this way, a good neighbourly relationship started to develop, a fact which was much appreciated by Maria.

The number of births continued to increase and, in addition, Maria was also more in demand as a nurse. She was extremely skilled and patient when she was dealing with children. She understood how to calm them and how to entertain them with a treasure trove of stories and fairy tales. They swallowed their medication, if it came from her hand, and they let themselves be rocked to sleep by her. She often sat for hours next to a small bed while little patients slowly dozed off, firmly holding onto one of Maria's fingers. Woe betide her if she, herself tired, tried to pull her finger ever so gently away — then, the baby would wake up with a start and the long procedure of getting the little patient to sleep had to begin all over again. Maria therefore always carried a small carrot in her apron pocket and pushed it, carefully substituting it for the finger, into the little fist as the sandman approached; this trick usually worked.

When people were seriously ill, she was often called to keep vigil for adults at night, just as her grandmother had done in the past, and this happened frequently with patients in hotels, too.

During the season she was therefore busy enough and often even overworked, but she enjoyed being a nurse and midwife very much, and was proud that her work was appreciated. Gone were the days when she sat in the kitchen in the evening, despairing and wondering whether she would be able to get the rent for the house together in time.

Nevertheless, she continued to take on day jobs whenever possible, particularly during the spring and autumn months, the so-called 'dead season'. She helped villagers with their cleaning, ironing, mending and laundry — often after a long night vigil at the bedside of a sick patient.

Her mother, too, contributed to the upkeep of the family by working in different households, mostly for the ladies next door. The small rent she received for the 'chestnut cottage' in the Val Bregaglia, which Lisabetta had inherited from an aunt, represented some welcome additional income. This rent consisted of a bag of dried chestnuts, which enriched the menu in the winter.

Furthermore, Lisabetta received a bundle of raw wool, which she spun in the evenings, sitting on the oven bench in the warm living room, while telling Rudolf and Nina stories about the past.

Maria knelt in the wash house with the ever cheerful Pierina, lathering, scrubbing, and rinsing the bedding, undergarments, aprons, towels and other laundry in the waters of the Inn. These were long hard days. She was with the families early in the morning, before seven o'clock, loading a small cart with the dirty washing, soap, brush and tubs. The large pieces had to be washed by midday, so that they could be spread out to be bleached on the meadow next to the riverbank. The work was not usually finished before seven o'clock in the evening, with only a short break for lunch. The pay for the whole day's work was one franc and twenty centimes. That was the local rate, which applied to Celerina and in the villages around.

Maria thought that this was simply not enough. That a long and exhausting working day like this was rewarded with such a small amount made her truly angry. No man, not even the most useless, unskilled skivvy would have turned up for such a ridiculous sum.

She could not get it out of her mind and she asked all the laundresses to come to her house one evening. After serving them a good cup of coffee and some cake, she explained her plan to them.

'We really have to demand more pay. The work is strenuous and unhealthy when it is cold, and — let us face it — everything has become more expensive in the last few years, and the wages of farmhands and labourers have, after all, also been increased. It is simply unfair to ignore us women and let us slave away on our knees, with our hands in cold water, for one franc twenty centimes. We have to ask for one franc fifty — that is the minimum. We shall only succeed, though, if we all, without exception, agree on this rate and stick to it. If even one of us does not join in, the whole thing will fail.'

Pierina, who was acknowledged to be the best and most popular laundress in the whole village, was immediately enthusiastic. Others had doubts. What if the housewives said no and they ended up with no work at all?

'Well, we shall have to stick together; that is the only way it will work', Maria explained.

Pierina came to the point.

'If we all insist on this rate, the women must accept it. Or do you perhaps think that they would themselves come down here to the Inn and do their own laundry?'

This made sense, and unanimously they decided to raise the daily rate for cleaning to one franc fifty centimes, too.

The women kept to their agreement and they told their surprised customers the next day that a washday was going to cost them one franc fifty and that the same applied for a cleaning day. This caused quite a commotion in the village. What on earth did these laundresses think they were doing, making such demands? Nothing like this had ever happened; this was indeed unheard of. It was discussed in all the houses where women were employed at a daily rate. The ladies got together, asked who might be behind this rebellion and felt that they really would not have to put up with this, and that they would simply refuse to play along. This continued until an unbiased husband, who happened upon the ladies' gathering as they were discussing the laundresses' revolt, chimed in with the question about whether one of them wanted to do the laundry down at the Inn herself.

Reacting to the shamefaced silence he added, 'As far as I know, this is now the rate all laundresses demand and they are actually right. One franc fifty is not too much for such heavy work; they could even ask for more, in fact.'

At that, he was greeted with resounding protest. Finally, however, the ladies gave in and everyone agreed the fee demanded. In the evening of the washing day, the money was handed to each laundress — albeit with a slightly sour expression, but after a few months there was no mention of it anymore.

Maria heard only rarely from Padruot and what she heard was usually bad news. He always reported when his illness flared up, episodes which were normally followed by the loss of his job. He also informed her about his physical weakness and other difficulties, as well as about the generally bad times. Maria was aware how well she, Lisabetta and the children were, despite the hard work, which often included night shifts, when she kept vigil for patients. This way it was even possible for her to send money to her sick husband.

Admittedly, Lisabetta silently shook her head at that, but Maria said, 'He is my husband, after all, and the father of my children.'

Every now and then she worried about the house. She knew little about the family of the three sisters. They had mentioned that they had relatives in France, and that was what concerned her. What if these relatives were to assert a claim on the house that had become their home? Not inconceivable. The sisters would not terminate the rental agreement, but family ties might perhaps have priority. In any case, they had to keep their eyes open for other options, because it was still difficult to find apartments. It was in reality out of the question; the flats there were too expensive.

The demand for accommodation rose in other villages, too, particularly since there was talk of building a railway from Chur to the Engadin. Planning was already underway and the financing of such a project was a constant topic among the regulars in the pub and in local and regional papers.

Maria's preferred option was to stay in Celerina, not only because of its central position, but also because the population had welcomed her and her family so warmly. This was the place where she felt at home; her children went to school here, and she had found safety and the feeling of security here.

Maria knelt in the wash house at the Inn and rinsed the bedding of the three sisters, for whom she had taken on this rather onerous chore. Next to her, Pierina started washing her customers' shirts with lots of soap. The work went easily for both of them, and shortly before the midday bells tolled, they were ready to hang up the clean laundry. They watched the wagtails, which were hopping from rock to rock along the riverbank, their tails bobbing up and down, as their name implies.

Pierina said, 'Have you got time in the afternoon? Shall we go into the Stazerwald and look for mountain cranberries? You know how healthy they are. I am making them into jelly — I am particularly fond of it, because it is not so sweet.'

Maria said that there was so much to do in the house, now that she was not busy with patients or new mothers for once, but Pierina pre-empted a possible objection with the following words, 'Tear yourself away. In the house you can always find work that should be done, but we should both enjoy such a beautiful warm afternoon. Come along!'

She was right. Moreover, Lisabetta had recently announced that the stock of preserved cranberry was running low and a few additional jars would definitely come in useful. Thus, Maria and Pierina went out in the afternoon.

The sun stood in the west and poured its rays over Celerina when the women, each with a basket full of berries, approached the village on the path from Stazerwald. The village lay peacefully in the evening sunshine and Maria thought, 'How beautiful this dear little place is.' Although it was not normally in her nature to burden other people with her troubles, she told Pierina her worries about the house.

Thoughtfully, Pierina tilted her head.

'I do not believe that the sisters would throw you out. They are quite strong-willed, certainly Giuditta is, and they will not be easily influenced by others. Admittedly, I do not know their relatives, nor what they are like or how much influence they have.'

She pointed out the old house, which lay opposite the wash house at the end of the lane towards the river, from which it was separated only by a garden and the field path, and said, 'To have your own house is always good, for example, one like that over there.'

Maria had never seen anyone living in that house, ever since she had moved to Celerina. The shutters were closed, the garden was overgrown and wild. She knew that it belonged to a citizen of Celerina who had moved to Italy, but he obviously never visited his home country.

Deep in thought, she said to Pierina, 'What a pity that this fine house is always shut up. I cannot understand at all why people who own such a place never come here, not even during the summer, when it is so beautiful down here on the Inn.'

'Well, you know, Carlo the owner wanted to refurbish his house years ago so that he could move into it in his old age. He arranged for two old windows to be replaced by big beautiful new ones, as is the fashion nowadays. And there are already new shutters, and inside the house, in the large attic space, he planned to build two new rooms. The frames are there, but then all work stopped, because his wife, an aristocratic lady from Siena, declared that she would never live in this cold country. A winter in the Engadin — that was completely out of the question, such freezing temperatures and a wilderness without culture, without concerts and theatres.[20]

'Years have passed since then, nobody comes any more, not even in the summer, and the house has remained shut. This is a sin, particularly given that there are many people looking for apartments. That could be a house for you, could it not? I shall have to show it to you some time. I have the keys, because I am still responsible for looking after the house, and it is due an inspection soon, in any case.'

'It is out of the question for me to buy a house. I am just glad to have a roof over my head and can only hope that this will remain the case for a long time.'

'Yes, yes, I know, but I would still like to show it to you. Come over this time tomorrow and we shall have a look at it.'

The inner, 'day' door turned with a creak in the big entrance gate, when Pierina entered the house with Maria the next day. A strange silence overcame them, the musty smell of houses that had been closed for a long time; an abandoned dwelling where people had once lived, cried and laughed, where they had talked and been silent. In short, where there had been life.

---

[20] Translated from the original Italian "senza cultura, senza concerti e teatro".

Pierina pushed the shutters open and Maria discovered that the large corridor, the so-called sulèr,[21] had two windows overlooking the lane. The kitchen, with its vaulted ceiling, was long and rather narrow. On one side, a window opened up towards the south and, beneath it, there was the sink, which was carved out of one great big stone. On the other side, there were a bench and a long table, and in the corner, hanging from a hook, were the copper kettles for the water from the fountain. From the kitchen, there was access to the big, cool pantry in the north-east corner, with several shelves and a table, and right next to it, there was another, bigger, chamber with a window. Then came two steps down into the low-ceilinged living room.

While Pierina pushed the shutters open, talking non-stop, Maria became very quiet. They found themselves in a simple little room, as in most farmhouses in the Engadin, but it was lovely, cosy and friendly. Two of the narrow hopper windows looked out towards San Gian, the church across the fields, and the south-west. To the left of the door stood the massive stove with its homely bench and the little doors with intricate patterns above the stone. Between the stove and the wall, the so-called 'burel',[22] a few small, narrow steps led upstairs. The walls were panelled, and there was a bench seat running underneath the windows.

Maria went up to one of the windows and looked across the Inn and the meadows towards Pontresina, the forest with the dark mountain pines and the bright golden larch trees and the flat grassland on which the cattle were grazing, having returned to the valley only a few weeks ago.

---

[21] The 'sulèr' is a hallway used as a work or storage space for equipment on the ground floor of typical Engadin houses.
[22] The 'burel' is a narrow little staircase, which leads through a trapdoor into the bedrooms upstairs.

Above it all, there was the deep blue sky. This picture of quiet beauty sank deep into Maria's heart. How happy the residents of this house should be.

'What do you say?' Pierina asked with pride, as if she were advertising her own possession.

'Oh, Pierina, I had not imagined it to be so beautiful and cosy. It would be wonderful to live here, but I do not believe that I could ever buy something like this. I shall never have that much money.'

'You have to look at the rest, too. Come.'

The 'rest' were two interconnected rooms upstairs, which were heated by warm air from the oven in the living room through a flap and then, on the same floor, the shell of the two rooms that had been started. Apart from that, there was nothing all the way up to the roof. The gable façade was made of beams with cracks so big that light could penetrate and which would obviously not keep out wind and weather.

In the rear part of the house, extending from the ground to right under the roof, there was the hay barn made of curved wooden planks set into the walls to allow for good circulation. In the basement, there were two cellars and low stables, each with separate spaces for large livestock and small domestic animals.

'Down here', Pierina said, 'unfortunately, the house is occasionally flooded. When there is too much water in the Inn, the ground water rises and the water covers the whole cellar shoe-deep. And sometimes even higher, but', she added quickly, 'it has never risen all the way up to the ceiling of the cellar.'

In the evening, Maria told her mother about her visit to the house next door. Lisabetta said that it had crossed her mind — whenever she looked across — that she would love to live there. She was, of course, happy that the sisters let their house to them, but she also often thought what might happen when there were changes in the old ladies' circumstances.

'At the moment, this is not the case and so it is doubtless best if we forget about it for the time being and go to bed.'

The winter season was over again and everyone was content. The hotels had been busy throughout, with profits exceeding those of the previous year, as the local press reported with satisfaction. Now was the time to shutter the windows and put the sign 'Closed until 1 June' at the hotel entrance. Tranquillity moved into the Engadin.

It was getting dark when Lisabetta, coming from the dairy, approached the gate with her milk pail and was surprised by a man wearing a cape and a hat, which was pulled right over his forehead. She asked, slightly confused, whether he was looking for something. With a strangely broken voice the man explained that he was looking for Duonna Maria and appeared as though he were about to enter the house. Lisabetta quickly stood in the doorway and said, 'Just a moment. I shall get my daughter.' With that she turned to the inside of the house and called Maria.

'Lisabetta', the man suddenly gasped, 'do you not know me?'

Lisabetta tried in vain to recognise the man in the dark. He behaved oddly and now he started swaying in a way that made her think he was drunk.

'What do you want, Sir? Who are you?' she asked.

Before the man could answer, Maria came. She stepped closer, hesitated, looked into the man's face.

'It is you...'

'Maria'. It sounded like a sigh.

He appeared to want to say something else, but his voice failed and he teetered even more.

Maria grabbed his arm fast.

'You are sick.'

Putting two fingers on his neck, she said, 'You have a temperature. Come inside. Mamma, make a fire and put the kettle on.'

The man then slumped onto the bench behind the kitchen table and sat there. He looked pitiful, his face caved in, his eyes shining feverishly, his thin body shuddering and his teeth chattering. Maria had fetched a blanket from the living room and put it around his shoulders. In silence, she prepared coffee for him and put a steaming cup on the table in front of him. He picked it up with trembling hands and carefully took a couple of sips of the hot drink.

'Could you please make the bed up in the little room next to the pantry and put a hot water bottle into it? Leave the doors open so that the warm air from the kitchen can circulate and heat it up a bit', Maria asked her mother, adding some wood to the logs in the fireplace.

Lisabetta went over to the little room and while she prepared the bed, she caught fragments of the conversation between her daughter and this stranger.

'I could not bear it anymore. I am sick, sick, sick.'

'I can see that. Tomorrow I shall call the doctor.'

'No, no. I shall get better here by myself.'

'You need a doctor, that is obvious to me and I have enough experience in such matters.'

Maria was now quite the professional nurse and declared firmly, 'Tomorrow the doctor will be called!'

The voices quietened down, until Lisabetta heard the man shout, 'I could not care less. What will be will be. All I can do is live here now and if that cannot be, I can at least die here and be buried in San Gian.'

Maria seemed to calm the situation down. Lisabetta could not understand the words, and her daughter appeared immediately afterwards and led the man into the room. To her mother she said, 'Please go upstairs and try to sleep. I am coming in a moment.'

The following morning Maria turned to her children over breakfast and said, 'Padruot has returned. He is very ill. I have put him to bed next door and shall make sure that the doctor will visit later on today.'

'Who is Padruot?' Rudolf asked puzzled.

Lisabetta seemed to want to say something, looked towards Nina and Rudolf and then closed her mouth again. The two women exchanged a glance. How should they explain the sad truth to the children?

'Padruot is your father; he has lived in Italy until now. And now he is back here.'

Nina had already understood the situation the evening before and would have liked to know more, but the concerned expression on her mother's face had stopped her asking questions. Even now she did not wish to ask. It was too obvious that their father's return worried her mother. Maria did not like to talk about the ill-fated story of the collapse of the firm and their father's escape, and had briefly informed Nina and Rudolf only on one occasion.

There followed an extremely difficult time. Padruot was in bed for many weeks, repeatedly shaken by severe attacks of fever, which left him totally exhausted. Despite his resistance, Maria had called the doctor. His treatment, and the intensive care Maria gave him, gradually reduced his temperature and his strength slowly returned, too. He managed to get out of bed, regained his appetite and Dr Bernhard thought that he would be well enough to start working again.

It took Maria a lot of effort, and only after many hours of discussion could she convince him to give himself up to the authorities. He was told that the matter was past the statute of limitations. Moreover, after the bankruptcy, the power station had been sold to the corporation of spa hotels in St Moritz, which meant that the debts had been mostly paid off.

'And then the corporation immediately installed a power cable to Silvaplana, for which they had not wanted to fork out money before, when they should have bought electricity from me; and now they become rich with what has been taken from me.'

This sounded extremely bitter, desperate indeed. Maria sympathised; she had, after all, felt the impact of the collapse, too.

When Padruot's health had stabilised somewhat, he started looking for work. Fortunately, he soon found a job in the electricity station at the end of the Inn gorge. The small, simple plant, which had been built several years before, no longer satisfied demand, and the successful hotelier who owned that installation therefore decided to build a facility with enhanced technical capabilities.

Padruot's expertise and experience were now in demand and he was employed. He observed, not without resentment, how important and precious electricity and its production had become — that he had been right with his plans, could be seen very clearly.

Time and again, he suffered from attacks of fever, but they were not as severe and normally did not last as long as during the first period after his return, which meant he had to take fewer days off sick.

Maria had many new mothers in her care, because a growing number of people visited the Engadin. The number of inhabitants increased in the villages, resulting in more births. New buildings mushroomed everywhere and even the simplest rooms in a farmhouse could be rented out during the season; tourists were often content to sleep on a hay-covered barn floor.

The whole valley experienced what seemed like an almost improbable boom. In the summer, the existing hotels burst at the seams, but in the winter, too, there were many more guests. It became fashionable to escape the fog in the lowlands and to enjoy oneself in snow and sun.

Even after the construction of the Grand Hotel in St Moritz — the biggest building in Switzerland and one of the most elegant hotels in the world — more luxury hotels were erected; only the best and latest would do for the spoilt guests.

St Moritz around 1900

Nina 1890–1975

Barba Gian,[23] her mother's brother, was beside himself. His dark eyes flashed brightly, and the ends of his black moustache stood up wild and unkempt.

'What, you want to allow Nina to work in an office? Surely she is far too young and inexperienced to be alone among all these men. How do you expect this to happen exactly?'

'It is very simple. She will use the skills she has learnt at school and will certainly learn some new ones. In any case, she is already enrolled in an evening course, as she will need shorthand', Maria said quietly.

Gian had travelled from Florence to Celerina for a short visit, to be at the funeral of a great-uncle of his wife Emilia. While she visited relatives, he sat in the kitchen with Lisabetta and Maria, and there was a lively exchange of news. Maria had mentioned that Nina, who finished school in the spring, had found a position in the office of 'St Moritz Tourism'.[24]

Gian was outraged.

'I cannot understand you, but I suppose I should have foreseen that this is where it would all end up, given that our village school was not good enough for you and that you thought she absolutely had to go to the secondary school in St Moritz.'

---

[23] 'Barba' means 'uncle' in Romansh.

[24] Most bigger mountain villages in Switzerland have a so-called 'Kurverein'. A Kurverein, here at St Moritz Tourism, is a local administrative authority that gives information and advice to tourists, for example on hotels, and ensures that facilities for holidaying guests, such as hiking paths, are kept safe and in order. The Kurverein is also responsible for collecting tourist taxes, either through hotels or directly from owners of accommodation which is rented out.

'It was her teacher at the school here in Celerina who advised me to send her to the new secondary school in St Moritz, where they teach foreign languages and typing. He said that she was an excellent and industrious student who should not miss out on the opportunities a good education could provide. That made sense to me; after all, I know well enough, how important it is to have a profession.'

'Oh, come on, she will get married just like any other girl, and what she has to know as a housewife and mother.'

'That she has learnt already. You know that; you have always praised her when you came to us, because she knuckles down and helps mother and me. She definitely has all the skills needed to run a family, and now she has also learnt French and English, and typing.'

'And you paid for three years to have her educated at this secondary school, as if you did not have to skimp already.'

'Of course I had to pay school fees, but I have not had to ask you for money, you will admit.'

'I offered, but you, with your pride, would never have accepted it', grunted Gian.

'It has not been necessary — so far we have muddled through without getting into debt.'

'Yes, yes, just like Mamma', said Gian and put his hand on his mother's shoulder, as she was listening silently to the altercation.

Now she turned to Gian and said resolutely, 'Maria is right. Nina must learn a profession.'

'But girls do not necessarily need a career. Which other girl in this valley has an occupation?'

'I am not interested in other girls', Maria interrupted. 'What I am interested in is the future of my children, and it

140

is for this that I am working. What others are doing is their business.'

Gian appeared unconvinced and wanted to add something, but Lisabetta interrupted by declaring, 'Nina has been offered this position and this is a unique opportunity. Do you want to spoil it for her?'

Gian shrugged his shoulders and grumbled something about stubborn women, but left it at that.

Only a few days after the end of school, Nina started her job at St Moritz Tourism. Slightly anxious and uncertain, she stood in front of the desk of Sar Alfred, the vice-president of the regional tourism authority. He sat there as if on his throne, cutting an imposing figure, with an awe-inspiring moustache and an authoritative voice. He was clearly used to being obeyed, and Nina was duly impressed.

Maria and Nina

'Reliability, accuracy and good manners, that is what we need here', he said briefly, 'and my informants have told me that you have these qualities. I have made enquiries, of course, and hope that this is indeed the case. And I shall now show you our office.'

With these words he led her into the information bureau, explaining to Nina that her main task would be to give information and advice to the guests.

'You will be able to do this; after all, you have grown up here.'

As a result, right from the first morning, Nina stood behind a counter with drawers full of brochures, hotel lists, programmes for sporting and cultural events and further information full of pictures. Nina advised the guests who came into the office as best she could without having been able to prepare herself properly.

Sar Alfred had made it plain that she had to read all this background material as soon as possible in order to be well informed. There was a lot to learn and Nina soon realised that she could hardly study all these papers during working hours as there was a continuous flow of people with questions and requests — and this was only the start of the summer season. Her sparse free time was thus fully occupied with reading marketing and information material. Many enquiries were particularly related to the spa in St Moritz Bad. There was extensive literature with medical analyses and explanations full of scientific terminology with which Nina was not familiar. She made a great effort, however, to get up to speed in this area, too, as Sar Alfred noted with satisfaction.

Apart from providing information, Nina was also in charge of collecting and dealing with the guest registration lists, which the hotels brought to her every morning. In addition, she had to answer the extensive correspondence, responding to letters on the basis of Sar Alfred's drafts, which were always written in pencil. After she had finished her shorthand course, she took dictation; Sar Alfred usually provided just some key words.

Nina soon settled in, got used to her boss's military style and took pleasure and interest in finding the information she had to communicate in response to the enquiries. Her tasks were varied, she encountered people from all over the world, had to attend to many different wishes and requests, and communicate in several languages. This was no problem for Nina, as she had a natural talent for languages.

As far as men went, Uncle Gian need not have been concerned. Apart from an older man, an employee of Sar Alfred's in the hotel, who came to the office once a week to check the cash and do the accounts, Nina had no contact with any of the men who were working there. Among them were workers who built the hiking trails and maintained the paths, the spa gardens and the flowerbeds in parks and public grounds. In winter, they were responsible for clearing the snow on the paths, but they also acted as 'icemen'. They produced the ice on the skating rink, made sure it was clear of snow and that it was sprayed with fresh water every evening, so that a mirror-like, glassy surface greeted the many guests who were keen skaters.

These workers reported for duty in front of the tourism office every Monday morning. Here they were given their schedule for the week ahead by Sar Alfred, in a sergeant major voice. On Saturday evenings they assembled again at the same place, where Sar Alfred handed each man his wages and issued praise and rebuke, with his voice echoing far and wide. Indeed, he was not too shy to administer a clip around the ear in special cases, which made Nina, who was observing this through the open door, wince.

The construction of the Rhaetian Railway from Chur into the Engadin brought a miraculous boom to St Moritz and the surrounding villages. More hotels and villas with luxury apartments were built. Public facilities were continuously improved, and the range of sporting and cultural events extended.

It soon became obvious that the current structures of the existing authority were no longer sufficient to deal with the new situation. A local tourist office for St Moritz was founded to take over from the regional tourist office, which covered the whole of the Upper Engadin. The Protestant vicar was appointed president. He was cosmopolitan, full of initiatives and progressive in his attitudes. In a short space of time, he turned the rather modest organisation into a modern institution. They employed more staff; for example, a man to deal with the ever-growing number of brochures, posters, advertisements and similar documentation, as well as someone to maintain and control the equipment for the workers. In addition, a new employee had to be found to supervise the group of workmen, whose number had also increased over time. Accounts and event-planning, as well as extra help on the information desk, were areas where additional full-time staff members were needed.

Mr Diethelm, who had worked in a local travel agency, was appointed to this position. He was an educated, widely travelled, articulate man in his early thirties who — in his capacity as accountant for Wagon-Lits, the international sleeping car company — had visited all the big cities in Europe and Russia.

It was a pleasure to work with him. He was a gentleman who treated his young colleague and his subordinates with the same courtesy as the illustrious guests. As a keen walker and mountaineer, he had already learnt his way around St Moritz and the surrounding area. Even when he was still working for the travel agency, he had often volunteered as a helper when events had to be organised, so that this aspect of his work was already familiar to him.

Guests arrived from every European country. In the Tourism Office, it was obvious that guests had to be attended to in their native languages. Nina, who spoke German as well as Romansh, got by with the French she had learnt at school and with the English, which she had improved by attending evening courses. Her Italian, too, was good enough to talk to customers, although it was clearly influenced by the Italian dialects spoken in the neighbouring valleys and also by her native Romansh. However, she needed foreign languages for her written work as well, for while Mr Diethelm was responsible for English and French correspondence, he had no Italian, so this became one of Nina's duties. She realised fairly soon that her written Italian was not good enough.

It was therefore a stroke of luck that Uncle Gian, who now lived in Italy, was on a visit to his mother and sister. After finishing his apprenticeship as confectioner and pastry cook in Rouen, he had moved to Italy — his boyhood dream — and found a job in a cake shop. The owner, a competent professional, liked his new, young, hardworking and ambitious employee. As he himself was already of a certain age and did not have any children, he took Gian on as a partner after a few years. Not long thereafter, he decided to retire completely and to sell Gian his firm. Gian devoted himself with all his strength and total commitment to the business and soon turned it into an even more successful concern. He had remained faithful to the love of his youth in Celerina, the pretty, slim Emilia with her fair skin, blonde locks and blue eyes. She, too, came from a respected family and had stayed true to the tall, dashing and lively Gian. Despite great opposition from her family, they married after Gian had properly settled in Florence. Now he was a successful businessman and could offer his wife and their two sons, who had arrived in the meantime, the life of a well-off family, with a large apartment and servants in the best neighbourhood.

He had come to terms with the fact that Nina worked in the tourist office, as he could see for himself, every time he came to the Engadin, that her job was interesting and fairly well paid, and that Nina remained the same quiet, friendly girl she had always been.

'So that is what you do in this office. Quite interesting, I have to admit, and you appear to be in your element with these Germans and Englishmen', he said, when he turned up at her work one day and observed for a while what was going on.

Nina smiled, 'Yes, I enjoy having to use foreign languages. Communication with the French and Italian guests is quite straightforward, though I have to write in Italian, too, and that is a bit of a problem. I definitely need to work on improving it. If only I knew how to go about it.'

Gian thought for a short time and said, 'You would learn how to write Italian most quickly in Italy and the best place would be Florence, where Dante's language is spoken. You could live with my family and I would make sure that you take lessons, so that you would have a firm grasp of the written language, too.'

Nina was ecstatic about the suggestion — the prospect of travelling to Florence was so tempting. Barba

Gian, his wife Emilia and their two sons were always raving about Florence when they visited their old home in the summer.

But then she started to have concerns. Surely she could not simply stay away from work for a long period. What would they say in the tourist office about such a plan?

'Why do you not ask your president? If he keeps mentioning the importance of good written Italian for your correspondence, as you tell me, then he ought to give you the opportunity to learn it. How about taking, say, three or four months off during the low season, for example, between the end of February to the end of May. That might be enough if you study hard in Florence.'

Nina looked uncertainly at her beloved and adored uncle, but promised to talk with the president.

On one of the following days, she gathered all her courage and laid Uncle Gian's proposal in front of her manager. To her surprise he thought it was an excellent idea and urged her to go ahead, if possible during the coming spring.

With his by now typical generosity he decided at once, 'You can add June to your stay and that should then be enough for you to learn to write Italian well, as you are already quite good at speaking it. I do, of course, expect great commitment on your part.'

Thus it was a done deal. Before he returned to Florence, Gian promised to make all the necessary arrangements for the language tuition.

The long journey and the stay in this wonderful city would be an unforgettable experience for Nina, which was to remain with her forever as a vivid memory.

On 1 March, she travelled by mail coach from St Moritz to Chiavenna, in her hand the wicker basket, in which she carried all her luggage. In Chiavenna, she changed to the railway and arrived by night train in Florence, tired, but full of impressions from her trip. Uncle Gian was waiting for her at the station, and they took a coach to his apartment, which was in a massive old house on the bank of the Arno.

The house was completely silent. Everyone was already asleep, but next morning she was warmly welcomed by Aunt Emilia and her two cousins, who immediately monopolised her. She had to admire their rooms and all their beautiful toys. Nina was deeply impressed by the size of the apartment and, above all, the height of the rooms and the fact that there was a servant to do the housework and a plump, good-natured cook, who reigned in the kitchen.

A room had been prepared especially for Nina, in which there was — apart from the bed and wardrobe — a table under the window, where she could study.

In the next few days, Uncle Gian took time to show Nina his city's most important and beautiful buildings. The girl could hardly comprehend how one could build churches as enormous as the cathedral and other places of worship, and how they could be fitted out in a way otherwise known only from fairy tales. The broad streets and the wide pavements, which were covered with big light-coloured stone slabs, fascinated her just as much as the bridges, particularly the Ponte Vecchio with its multitude of small shops where, it seemed to Nina, treasures from all over the world were on offer.

She was no less impressed by Uncle Gian's shop. Thanks to his ability, he had become extremely successful. A small cake shop had turned into a large enterprise, including a café much frequented by high society, in a prime location on the Piazza del Duomo. A good number of staff, among them several young people from the Engadin, were employed there. All of this meant that Gian's family could afford to live in some comfort. It was no secret that Nina's uncle was proud of his achievements, not least because he — the son of a poor widow — had not been acceptable to Emilia's family and only the tenacity of the two lovers had finally conquered the initial resistance.

As early as the fourth day, Professore Virgilio, a friend of Gian's family, turned up after lunch for the first Italian lesson. He was an elderly gentleman, a retired professor, slightly awkward, but a real master of his language.

The students he had taught over the years had perhaps been too young to appreciate his abilities. Now he had one who was a little more mature and therefore more knowledgeable, and who was, above all, very much aware that she had to use the time at her disposal wisely. Nina was determined to learn as much as possible during these four months. Listening to Professore Virgilio, when he explained the grammatical rules in his melodious Tuscan Italian and quoted from the works of poets, preferably from Dante's *Divina Commedia*, gave Nina a lot of pleasure and she always followed his lessons with great attention.

When the professor left after two-and-a-half hours — though he often stayed longer — Nina sat down to her homework and did not allow herself to be disturbed, not even by the two boys, when they burst into her room and tried to get her to play with them. Instead, she devoted herself to them in the morning, which Aunt Emilia appreciated very much, as this enabled her to go shopping in the market with the cook, without being disturbed.

Emilio and Rudolf were extremely lively boys and always ready for pranks — making her way through the crowded market with these two rascals was extremely exhausting. They constantly tried to escape and that caused a lot of fuss and hassle until they could be found again in the crowd of people. Aunt Emilia panicked each time and that was, of course, exactly what the two troublemakers enjoyed.

Now that Nina was there, she sat with them in the dining room, told them stories and talked about life in the mountains. Emilio and Rudolf could never hear enough about the daily routine in winter, when the wooden ploughs piled up the snow so high on the side of the road that children could not see over the walls.

'And every morning a path to the main door has to be shovelled clear and that is the task of the children in all families. On the way to school their feet get wet, because often only a narrow track has been made passable by people trampling past, but in these conditions children have snowball fights and jump from the fences into the deep snow, sinking so far that they become invisible. The big boys build tracks for sledges on the San Gian Church hill and on the steep fields of Provuler, north of the village too, and it is great fun to whizz down as fast as lightning', Nina reminisced.

She also told them about the strange foreigners who enjoyed tobogganing on iron sledges called 'bobs' or 'skeletons'.

'They swish through icy snow canals on the side of the road from St Moritz to Celerina on these heavy things, so fast that they make the air whistle.'

On Sundays, Nina walked through the beautiful city and its suburbs with Gian's family, through the splendid houses with their park-like gardens where trees that she had never seen before grew. There were palm trees and plants with huge leaves and, particularly now in spring, full of the most breathtakingly beautiful blossoms. Nina was taken on excursions to Siena, Pisa and Lucca, too. Her big eyes marvelled at the sights and she often thought that her heart could not comprehend so much beauty. When Uncle Gian took this child of the mountains to the beach and showed her the immense expanse of water, which somewhere — far away — gradually merged with the sky, she was excited beyond words.

Her stay in Italy was a precious time, full of enthralling impressions and unforgettable experiences, but also working hard on her Italian. Nevertheless, Nina was glad to return to the Engadin at the end of June, back to her loved ones, and to her job. She showed even more commitment in the summer, happy and grateful that her colleagues had made it possible for her to learn Italian, while spending such a fantastic and eventful time in Florence. In addition, her salary had been increased, because she was now fluent in another foreign language and this made it possible for her to stay in St Moritz for lunch and eat in the Hotel St Moritzerhof, where Herr Diethelm had his lunch, too.

In the meantime, Rudolf had finished school as well. Just like his father, he was passionately interested in everything related to electricity. Only in this area did he see his future career. He often talked about it with his sister. However, given his father's experience, he did not dare to talk about this dream to his mother. It was therefore Nina who mentioned it to her mother one day. To her surprise, she understood, even though she sighed, 'It has to be admitted, this new invention has not yet brought us much luck.'

She had long suspected that Rudolf did not wish to follow any other career than this one and she knew that he was a talented technician. She therefore tried hard to find the perfect training place for him and succeeded in locating a large electrical engineering firm in the French part of

Switzerland. This meant, of course, that she had to pay for his maintenance in addition to the cost of the apprenticeship. Barba Gian shook his head when he heard of it — was it not enough to learn a trade in the Engadin?

Many others in the village shared this view.

On her return home one evening, Nina found her mother in floods of tears in the kitchen. Grandmother Lisabetta was clattering around in the big larder next to it. It was obvious from the rough way she handled crockery, pots and pans that something must have occurred to provoke this exceptional fury. This was so unusual that Nina was very worried, the more so because her mother did not want to say what had happened.

Only late in the evening, when Lisabetta and her father had already gone to bed, did Nina sit with her mother in the living room and insist that she be told what was going on. At last, Maria opened up. She had visited the family of the head of the village to do their ironing, when the master of the house returned home and said cheerfully, 'I hear you have your own house now — congratulations!'

'No such luck', Maria had retorted laughing, 'this is something I have been dreaming of for a long time.'

'Well, now it has happened. I am serious.'

'What do you mean? I do not have a house.'

'But it is the truth — your husband bid for Sar Carlo's house earlier today and bought it.'

Maria reported sobbing that she simply could not bring herself to believe it and lost her composure completely. Sar Linard had to explain to her several times that the auction for Sar Carlo's house had taken place in the afternoon and that Padruot had made a bid and acquired it.

'I cried like never before, particularly not in front of other people. How could Padruot do something like this?

After all, he has no money. Sar Linard and his wife made every effort to console me, but they could not help me either.'

'Right, and what was father's reaction?' Nina wanted to know.

'He said that he had only gone to the auction out of curiosity and to listen, when he had seen it advertised on the village notice board. And then, he did not know why, he put his hand up once. Everyone fell silent, nobody continued bidding, and the auctioneer hit the table with his hammer and declared the house his property — for 13,000 Swiss Francs.'

'Is this all? Has he not got another explanation? How does he plan to pay for this? He has not got anything, surely. Have you made this clear to him?'

'Of course I have told him that, and much else on top. He simply kept silent, repeated a few times that he did not know what had overcome him. You know what he is like: he remains quiet, shrugs his shoulders and retreats to his room. It is impossible to talk to him. He just goes away. And then he said that we had always been so enthusiastic about this house and so keen to own it. He claimed he knew that I had once looked at it with Pierina. Surely that was proof enough that I had always wanted it.'

'And look! Now you have it.'

Maria started crying again. Nina could not hold back the tears either.

What in heaven's name should they do? Their thoughts were all over the place: something had to happen, but however hard they tried, they could not find a solution.

'Can this mad purchase not be annulled?'

'Sar Linard is afraid that this is almost impossible. In any case, it would be very expensive and there might be suspicions that Padruot had intentionally committed fraud, which might, of course, have legal implications — the more so because the matter of the power station in Silvaplana and also his escape at the time could resurface and raise more problems. Indeed, Sar Linard advised me to try to keep the house, saying it was a good property. In addition, he mentioned that we might not always be able to rent the sisters' house, as there was no guarantee what would happen to their house when the circumstances of the three women changed. Doubtless, the best solution would be for me to take on the house. But how can I do this? I certainly have not got enough money', Maria finished, totally disheartened.

Sleep will not have come easily to any of the three women that night. The hopelessness of the situation, the shame, the mockery of the people, all the difficulties which would return did not allow them to rest. Nina, too, tossed and turned sleepless in her bed. The fact that her father had put his family into such a desperate position for the second time made her bitter. Having spent her childhood without him — she could barely remember the years before his escape, as she had been so little at the time — she had not succeeded in creating a close bond with him, particularly as he increasingly withdrew himself when he was at home. He stayed in his room and only turned up at mealtimes to eat with the others. Even then, he was taciturn and hardly ever joined in conversations.

After her agitation and outrage had worn off a bit, she started to think hard. Somehow a solution had to be found.

The next morning she was down in the kitchen early, even before her mother, and when she joined her, Nina presented her with the plan she had hatched during the night.

'We have to buy the house — Sar Linard is right.'

Maria wanted to object, but Nina did not allow her to speak.

154

'We put our savings together. You have put something aside and so have I', she said, not without pride.

'Then I will go to the bank and talk to the director. I know him well, as he is of course also a member of the Board of Directors in St Moritz Tourism. It is possible that he may give us a mortgage to cover the rest.'

'What on earth are you thinking of? This is mad. The little we can scrape together is not enough. We shall not get a mortgage with such a small amount of capital.'

'And if grandmother…?'

'Certainly not. She helped me when I desperately needed her, and I do not know what I would have done without her at that time. It is unthinkable to make her part with her hard-earned savings again; we simply cannot do that.'

'Apart from that, is there nobody who could help us? Any of your customers? You bend over backwards for them; you are available day and night when someone is ill for such a small salary. And they tell you time and again how much they appreciate you who worked night after night, keeping watch when someone was ill, and for whom you still do rough housework for a meagre daily wage and whose children you babysit — if none of them is prepared to lend you some money, I shall talk to our president. Perhaps he could give me a loan, which could be deducted from my salary in instalments.'

'No, I shall not allow that. To burden your future with debt — what on earth are you thinking? But I shall reflect on it. Perhaps one of my clients may have some sympathy for me. Not that I like doing it but, as Sar Linard says, the day will come when we cannot live in our current house.'

Maria's house in Celerina
On the roof, the windmill that her husband had built to supply the house with electricity

It turned out to be one of the most respected citizens of the village who gave Maria a loan which, together with her and Nina's savings, made it possible to get a mortgage from the bank. Maria had been very close to Sar Roman's family for many years. His four children had a rather delicate constitution and had often been sick, and Maria had always been on the spot, not only to watch over them at night, but also to tell them stories in order to calm the little patients down.

In the spring, when the redstarts had returned from the south, and after Sar Carlo's house had been thoroughly cleared and cleaned, the move took place.

Giuditta, Anna and Annetta shed a lot of tears when they had to say farewell, but they understood, of course. Maria had explained the situation to them and had reassured them, 'Nothing will change between us. We shall continue to be good neighbours, even if we live opposite and not next to each other, and you can call me and my mother any time you need help. I shall always be grateful that you let your house to me. I shall never forget your kindness.'

It took several days before every item was in its new place and the furniture was arranged just as she wanted it. Then it turned into the home Maria had always dreamed of: simple, but cosy, bright and pleasant. When the evening sun poured its red rays over the hill in the east and covered the church of San Gian, when the swallows darted backwards and forwards above the lapping waves of the river Inn before they settled down in their nests — having passed through the big gate to the hallway which was open day and night — when she gazed over her front garden where the colourful peas, in full bloom, climbed the trellis that separated the flowerbeds from the chicken run, and when the fragrance from mignonettes, phlox, stocks and camomile wafted over, Maria was still overcome by the miracle that all of this was hers, even though the dreaded prospect of having to pay the mortgage felt like something drilling in the back of her head.

'Oh Mamma', Nina said, standing next to her. 'If tourism continues to grow as it has done, if guests keep visiting in such numbers and we both have such a lot of work, then we shall not only be able to repay the interest, but even start on the mortgage. So far the house has made us quite a profit, has it not? We really do not have to worry.'

Nina was right about this. The purchase of the house turned out to be a good investment. Maria employed a local carpenter to finish the renovation of the two rooms, which were still being refurbished when they bought the house. He worked for them in his free time and suggested that he could be paid in instalments, at the end of each season. Fortunately,

157

they then managed to rent out these rooms practically throughout the whole year.

Not long afterwards, the same carpenter asked whether he could rent the large hay barn next to their house to set up his workshop. Maria was concerned because the walls consisted of simple planks with spaces in between to ensure that the hay was properly aired.

'Let me worry about that. I shall put panels over them and add a floor. After all, the barn is two storeys high. Upstairs will be suitable for me to store my wood, where it can dry well — I have thought about it all. This will come with costs, of course, and I can therefore only rent the barn if you do not charge me a high rent in the first few years.'

Maria agreed.

The small rent for the carpenter's workshop, together with that for the two rooms, amounted to sufficient income to ensure that Maria could pay the interest she owed on time. She was keen, however, to repay Sar Roman's loan quickly.

The lodgers — young men who were professionals in the booming construction industry — soon pleaded with her to let them eat in her house, arguing that someone was cooking for the family in any case, and surely it would make not much difference to cook for two more, and they would, of course, pay a reasonable price. Maria was a good cook and Lisabetta, too, knew how to make a tasty meal with simple ingredients, and thus they started feeding two boarders as well. It did not take long before word got around to the colleagues of the two surveyors, and in the end, there were usually about four to six young men at the table during mealtimes, all of whom much appreciated the culinary skills of the two women.

Maria was careful to ensure that she was able to come home over lunch time, if necessary leaving a new mother for a short while, because she did not want to entrust all the cooking to Lisabetta, who was over seventy by then. Only in exceptional cases, for example during a birth, when the midwife had to stay with the woman, was Lisabetta alone in the kitchen. Apart from those occasions, the two women worked side by side, and this new source of income allowed them to forget the initial problems and reduced the debts. Nina, too, was relieved that the financial burden of the house purchase was noticeably shrinking, as it had been her, after all, who had eventually convinced Maria to buy the house.

The sullen, almost hostile atmosphere at home depressed her all the more, though. Her father, with his unstable health, had become increasingly aloof and grumpy. Privately, he felt a certain satisfaction when he saw how the situation had progressed since they lived in their own house, but he never mentioned it, as it was clear to him, too, that it was entirely due to Maria and Nina that the adventure he had had with the auction ended as well as it did. The fact that the two of them seemed to be successful in everything they did, while his ventures failed, made him feel envious. He was jealous, too, that his Maria, much younger than him and a good-looking woman who moved with agility and grace, often received compliments from men. The lodgers courted her and, of course, Nina, too, and this was not good for his self-confidence. He was therefore often in a bad mood and gloomy, reproaching Maria for accepting the gallantry of these young men. He told her that he felt too old to behave like that and muttered that she would probably prefer a young chap to an old man. Maria did not enter into debate on the subject, retorting in a curt manner that he could no doubt see that she had no time to fool around in this way, given that he was the reason that she had to work almost all day and night.

Padruot's installation of a windmill, which produced electricity on the roof, however, caused a stir in the village. He had made it himself with all the necessary fittings and then rigged up the cables. Thus the living room, kitchen, corridor and the new rooms had electric lights — a luxury that could so far only be found in hotels. In turn, this aroused the envy of those who were still using kerosene lamps and candles, and it irritated the managers of the power station; they were not pleased that one of their own employees was competing with them. After some discussion, those responsible were at last convinced that using electricity in private houses might have a great potential benefit and should be tried and tested.

After a short time, the managers of the power station themselves, and some hoteliers who were keen on modern technology, approached Padruot with the suggestion that an operation running electrical boats on Lake St Moritz should be established. Padruot should set up the facilities necessary for such an enterprise. A business like this had, indeed, existed a few years before, and reports of this had been publicised in many newspapers. The two boats had, however, already been destroyed by fire in the second summer and the cause was never discovered.

Padruot was very enthusiastic at once. A company was founded, and Padruot was instructed to order everything that was needed for the construction and assembly of such boats in St Moritz. In addition, he had to ensure that the power supply was routed correctly. Padruot eagerly started with the work, drawing and calculating throughout the winter. The weight of the accumulators and the number of the passengers had to be adjusted to the buoyancy of the boats, and this was a particularly difficult problem.

In late winter, he was ready to build the boats in a shed, and by the start of July they were already operational. The sockets where the boats were plugged in overnight were located on the western shore of the lake near the riding school. This way, there was enough power for them to run during the day.

On 27 July, posters were put up attracting the attention of the locals and the tourists: 'The much-loved electric powered boats operate on Lake St Moritz during the summer, running all day, from 9 a.m. to 7 p.m. with a lunch break of an hour. They will stop at the following piers every half hour: Surpunt St Moritz-Bad — Meierei — Waldschlössli — Bahnhof[25] — Casino, with connections to each arriving and departing train. The electric boats represent a handy and cheap new addition to the transport system.' This was printed in large letters.

The first days were promising: everyone wanted a ride across the lake in an electrically powered, fast boat — not in the little slow boats with their sunroofs, which were propelled by Italian 'gondolieri'.[26]

The interest faded after a while, though, and the expected success did not materialise, possibly because the weather was often rainy and cool that summer. At the end of the season, it was apparent that the boats had run at a loss. It was hoped that the next summer would be better, but the financial hole had become even bigger by the end of the season. The company had to declare itself bankrupt. Padruot found himself in a most upsetting situation. Not only did he lose a large part of the wages he might have earned, but as the buyer of the materials needed to build the boats, he was in debt on that front, too. There was a fight about that and

---

[25] 'Bahnhof' means 'railway station'.
[26] 'Gondolieri' are the famous Venetian rowers.

one of the arguments was that the budget had been exceeded, even though the costs had never been exactly agreed in advance. Padruot had placed the order and was therefore legally responsible. He was again faced with a mountain of debt.

The world fell apart for Maria and Nina. These debts, for which Maria was jointly liable with her assets — that is the house — meant, in simple terms, that she would lose her home. Again, just as when they were buying the house, they found themselves staring into the abyss.

They weighed up all options but could not see a solution. Maria felt unable to face approaching Sar Roman once more. She tried to talk with those responsible in the boat company. They, however, decided to follow the letter of the law and insisted that the orders for the materials had been signed by Padruot. Thus, he was liable.

Maria went to the bank. The director showed a certain amount of understanding, but made it clear that his hands were tied, too, as he was accountable to higher authorities. The size of the mortgage needed was a problem that could not be solved by increasing the loan on the house, given the special circumstances. Maria knew well that he was hinting that this was the third such debacle.

In despair, Maria stressed, 'Look, not only have I paid the interest and amortisation punctually, but have also started repaying the mortgage, even though I arranged for renovations to be undertaken, which have, of course, increased the value of the house. In addition, my daughter Nina will help with the repayments.'

Having been given this assurance, the director agreed to recommend to his superiors that Maria's request for a further loan be granted.

When they received a positive response from the bank, Maria and Nina were, of course, relieved — but they were hardly full of joy, because they were aware that they would have to make do without a very great deal, to work hard, to accomplish even more and to save.

Nina stopped going to lunch in the St Moritzerhof, but instead hurried home on foot — to save the fare — and then returned to work, walking up the long path back to St Moritz. As Antonio's carpentry firm developed into an increasingly successful enterprise, Nina took on the accounts and dealt with the shop's clerical work. As a result, she sat over the books and invoices when she had finished helping in the kitchen. Thanks to additional nursing duties and night vigils for Maria, they managed to keep the house and even to diminish their debts over the next few years.

Lisabetta had grown ever thinner and smaller. She was keen to look after herself, so as not to be a burden to anyone, and therefore made sure she did her own housekeeping in a quiet and contented way until close to her end. A weakness forced her to stay in bed one day and she closed her eyes forever in the same week. Although she had lived unobtrusively, the whole village came to her funeral in the cemetery in San Gian. Maria planted two peony bushes on her grave and they bore the most beautiful white and pink blossom year after year.

'We have to say farewell after this season, a sad and melancholy goodbye, our hearts full of grief and sorrow, but also full of anger and shame about the breakdown of the much praised civilisation of the old Europe. War has brought this about. It broke the spirit of the summer season in the Engadin, which had been so promising this August, and thus also that of our paper, which is devoted to the portrayal of the vagaries of this life. We are now asking our readers and patrons for forgiveness and forbearance, indeed all wise men and women — even if they might not approve of our approach. We are of course aware that we must bow to circumstances; we pray with you, with all our guests and, in particular, with the whole of our fatherland, for divine guidance through this troubled time in the history of the world and we say to you, "See you again in the winter of 1914/15".'

This was what the *Engadin Express & Alpine Post*, the paper for holiday guests wrote in its editorial at the end of August 1914. War had broken out, and it would escalate into a world war. It would certainly not last longer than a few weeks, perhaps months — this was what people believed, and this was the message in the concluding sentence of the farewell letter.

A beautiful summer — and in August the fully occupied hotels were empty from one day to the next. What purpose did an institution like Engadin Tourism have now? They considered closing the office and Nina trembled in fear of losing her job. Without her wages, how could she make her contribution towards the repayment of the bank loan? Her mother's earnings were not sufficient to cover the agreed instalments, quite apart from the fact that her income would go down now because, in these hard times, some of Maria's customers would do without her help. Even though the two, who had been saving with an iron will and discipline, had stuck rigorously to the repayment schedule and had, on top of that, made additional payments, there was still a substantial mortgage on the house.

After the initial shock, which the news about the outbreak of the war and the rushed departure of many guests had caused, it turned out that despite the gloomy state of the world, not all guests were leaving the Engadin. A good number of 'strangers' remained in St Moritz, and in surrounding villages, too, some tourists stayed on. The services of Engadin Tourism were therefore still needed, and for the time being, Nina's job was secure. She had to carry out all the duties in the office herself, however, because Diethelm, like most men of his age, had to do military service on the border.

Over the past few years, Nina and Diethelm had become closer and they often went for walks and excursions together in their free time. They shared a love of nature, were both interested in flora and fauna, but also in all that happened in the world. When Diethelm talked about his many trips, about foreign cities and railways, a wider world opened up to Nina. He was a well-read man, they talked about poets and books, about painting and music. Increasingly, they realised that there was a harmony between them.

It was, nevertheless, slightly unexpected when Diethelm, after he had received the conscription notice, said to her, like the gentleman that he was, 'I would like to go home with you tonight and ask your parents for your hand — if you agree', he added, when he noticed that he had caught her unawares, before he realised that he had actually surprised himself, as well.

They both began laughing, as they became aware that despite the dark times they had started their shared future with a burst of laughter.

The parents in Celerina, too, were a bit surprised, but it had not escaped them, either, that a closer bond had developed between Nina and Diethelm. Under different circumstances it might have taken slightly longer to reach the formal stage in their courtship, but many other young couples were in the same situation and took the same step in a slightly hurried fashion. It was therefore not a time for grand speeches; instead problems of a practical nature were being discussed without delay.

There was no engagement party, no cards or invitations — simply sitting around the table the same evening, enjoying just being together, getting to know each other better and becoming familiar with the idea that their daughter was now engaged to this man who, admittedly, they had met before and about whom they had heard quite a lot. What would tomorrow bring? There was no way of knowing and it thus seemed right not to interfere with this unconventional manner of getting engaged.

'What shall I do with Buster?'[27] Diethelm asked before he went away. Buster was his small black German spitz. Nina offered to care for the little animal during his absence, as she got on well with him, but when she came to take him to live with her in Celerina, he refused to abandon Diethelm's bachelor flat. There was nothing to be done other than to leave Buster in his familiar surroundings and care for him there.

In his first letter from military service, Diethelm suggested that she could use his flat not only when she was on dog duty, but that she might also want to cook her lunch in his kitchen, so that she did not have to walk all the way to Celerina and back. And this turned into a long-term arrangement. After a while, Buster got used to accompanying her when she walked home to Celerina and, eventually, even deigned to stay there overnight.

---

[27] The dog is called 'Pussy' in the original German, but Buster seemed a better choice of name in English in the 21st century.

Nina and Diethelm 1918

Many of the hotels remained closed, but those who had risked opening for the winter season 1914/15 found that there were still foreign guests happy to stay. In this way, people from neighbouring countries had the chance of escaping, at least for a short time, the threats and general shortages in their devastated, war-torn countries. They were looking for peace and tranquillity in the mountains and often also recovery from illness and war wounds. Thus, a kind of commuting started again during the seasons, if at a much reduced rate. Admittedly, this was not enough for many hotels to stay in business and quite a number of firms had to be taken over by banks, which caused them and the owners substantial losses.

     Maria's lodgers had to report for military duty, too, and this resulted in a lack of income. Maria tried to let these rooms to holiday guests again and, surprisingly, every now and then, there were some who appreciated finding cheaper accommodation in private lodgings. Since most wanted to have meals, too, the cosy lounge served as a dining room for the guests at lunch and dinner times. The scarcity of the rationed provisions were quite a challenge for Maria's skills and creativity, but she had always been a good cook and her culinary arts were very much valued in these frugal times.

Word spread, with the result that guests from other private lodgings got in touch, and the lounge was fully occupied during meal times.

Catering for tourists meant that Maria's days were so full that she not only had to give up the daily work she was doing for her customers, but after a while she was also forced to quit her post as a midwife. It was with a heavy heart that she said goodbye to this profession but the local authority's decision to reorganise the midwifery systems made this step easier.

In the third year of the war, Padruot fell ill. He had become increasingly weak and was obviously in pain. It took a long time before he was prepared to see a doctor. And the diagnosis was devastating: cancer of the oesophagus. After months of terrible suffering, death came as a blessed release. He, too, was laid to rest in the churchyard of San Gian.

When the war finally ended in 1918, Nina and Diethelm had a very quiet wedding. They now lived in Diethelm's small flat. In October the following year, Nina had her first baby, a girl. They baptised her 'Anita'. She was an extremely delicate child who weighed less than five pounds[28] at birth. Nina did not have any milk herself and the doctor told the parents that Anita might not survive. Maria, who fortunately

---

[28] Less than 4 metric pounds, i.e. 2 kg.

had no guests during these weeks — between seasons — came up from Celerina and spent all day administering tiny spoonfuls of goats' milk, mixed with water, to the little creature, because she was allergic to cows' milk. She started to gain weight very slowly, and around Christmas time, the doctor pronounced, a little surprised himself, that she was no longer in any danger.

'If we want a family, we must not wait too long', Diethelm said, because he was, after all, forty-three years old by then. Marcella was born fourteen months after Anita and another eighteen months later, Raeto arrived.

In the meantime, the family had moved into a larger apartment, from where they had a beautiful view across the lake towards the mountains. A noisy brook separated the house from the edge of a little wood. Their quiet lane, which made for fantastic sledging in the winter, had four neighbouring houses with other children. A bit further up, there was a large carriage business and coach houses, with many horses, cows, sheep, pigs and chickens. Many birds and squirrels lived in the small forest, and on the banks of the stream, there were frogs and dragonflies. The children could block the water to create dams, making small lakes that they surrounded with little gardens. The whole environment was a children's paradise.

With the two little ones and Anita, who was often poorly, Nina was frequently overwhelmed. The daily grind with its constant interruptions caused by the children's needs and mishaps meant that much on her to-do list was left undone; the general chaos and the restless nights were a strain on her energy and she often felt totally drained. Admittedly, Diethelm helped wherever possible, when he was at home, but the hours he could spend with the family were few and far between, because the duties in the office took a great deal out of him and during the season he also had to work in the evenings and on Sundays.

Nina often longed for her work in the tourism office, for the well-ordered daily life, for the knowledge that she had dealt with all her duties conscientiously and properly. She also missed the contact with people from all over the world, using foreign languages, and the praise from her managers. Nina found it hard to cope with this completely different way of life, with the result that she often suffered physically.

It took several years before St Moritz recovered from the decline caused by the war. Highly respected families, who had invested their fortune in hotels, had to give up everything as lost. Companies and businesses that were dependent on tourism did not fare much better. The fact that many of the loyal guests had not survived the war, or had become impoverished, allowed little hope for the future.

Nevertheless, St Moritz Tourism pulled out all the stops, organised events, as in the past, ensured that hiking trails and all the facilities were put in order again, and, hesitantly at the beginning — only as far as the sparse resources permitted — started promotions in Switzerland and abroad. The beautiful countryside, the health-giving altitude and the spa were able to attract tourists again, and step-by-step, so-called 'good seasons' began to return.

In this time of recovery, Diethelm was offered an interesting position in the management of a building firm. Nina and he had many discussions about the advantages and disadvantages of such a career change. Diethelm had always been interested in the construction industry, and his activities in the tourism office were linked, if only to a small extent, to tasks in this sector. All the same, the maintenance of the facilities, the deployment and management of the workers, and the payroll were all to be his responsibility. He was tempted by this opportunity to extend his skills and even more by the fact that he would have more time for his family. He would not have to attend sporting and social events at all hours — Sundays and evenings would belong to his family again. At last they could go hiking again together, experiencing nature in all its richness and chatting with the children in the evenings. That was the decisive factor. Diethelm moved into the construction industry and Nina was content, even happy, about this.

Nina's brother Rudolf had found a job as an electrician with the Rhaetian Railway, after finishing his apprenticeship. He had returned with great joy to his village, not least because a girl was waiting for him there. After his marriage to Oliva, there was the question as to where they should live. As Rudolf was emotionally attached — with every fibre of his body — to the house in which he had grown up, he suggested to his mother that she might let them live in a part of it. It would no longer be possible to take in paying guests, but the rent that he would of course pay, would make up for the lost income. Nina was in favour of this proposal, and Maria therefore decided to give up her guesthouse business and to leave her house to the young couple. She kept one of the refurbished rooms for herself, but did not wish to be without work. It did not suit her to be idle and thus she accepted the offer to run the laundry section of the Hotel Cresta Kulm.

Every week, Nina took her children to see her mother in Celerina. She no longer lived in the house on the River Inn, but in a hotel high up in the village. When they first visited her, they were directed towards a long corridor on the ground floor, to a large room, where they found their Nona[29]

---

[29]'Nona' is the Romansh word for 'grandmother'.

with two young assistants standing at the table, which was covered with long white cloths. She was sorting, spraying, starching and ironing the laundry and it was clear that she loved to work with the beautiful hotel linen and the guests' precious personal items. Between seasons, she stayed with Rudolf's family — now including two little daughters, Olga and Nelly. She also regularly spent several weeks with Nina in St Moritz.

Tourism improved. Guests returned to the Engadin in great numbers. The economy of the valley recovered. The construction industry, where Diethelm worked, grew rapidly, as buildings shot up everywhere, particularly when St Moritz was awarded the Olympic Winter Games of 1928. This major event brought the town into the headlines and made it famous around the world.

Only a year later, however, the Wall Street Crash affected the world economy and thus also tourism — the number of overnight stays went down. The events in neighbouring Germany, which had always been very important for the success of tourism in St Moritz, caused further setbacks not long afterwards. Diethelm used to say, 'Tourism fluctuates as a business, as it depends on so many factors: weather, snow conditions and, more than anything, the economic and political situation in Europe.'

The crisis had an impact on the construction industry, too — there were fewer contracts. Fear for the future increased. The children, however, did not notice anything. All three enjoyed school, and during their time off their surroundings offered many options for adventures. When they were not playing or engaged in sport outdoors, they could sit for hours with their books — they had, after all, inherited their passion for reading from their parents and grandmother.

Christmas was approaching. The first snowflakes fell softly to the ground as the children returned from school in the afternoon. No sooner were they in the entrance hall, than they were greeted by the smell of roasted apples waiting to be gobbled up for tea. As usual at this time of the year, Maria was in St Moritz. She sat with Nina in the living room, busy sewing costumes for a nativity play, which was to be performed in church on the first Sunday of Advent. The mothers of the Sunday school children had taken on the duty of producing the actors' garments from plain lengths of material. Excited and curious, Anita, Marcella and Raeto burst into the room keen to see and try on the costumes. But what was happening to their mother? She was not answering their questions, barely looked up and it appeared as if her shoulders were twitching.

'What is it, Mamma? Is there something wrong with you?'

Nina shook her head and started sobbing.

All three stood there confused and turned to their grandmother.

'Is Mamma sick? What is wrong with her?'

Nona, as the children called her in Romansh, shook her head, got up, took a plate of apples out of the oven and went over to the kitchen. The children followed, subdued.

Grandmother put the plate on the table and said, 'Leave your mother in peace now; do not ask any more questions. Something has happened — we shall tell you later on. You will hear about it soon enough. This much I can tell you — none of the other children will wear a costume into which as many tears have been shed as into yours.'

Nina's family in 1926, left to right: Raeto, Nina, Anita, Marcella, Diethelm

The children were startled and unsettled, because their mother had tear-stained eyes the next day, too. Papa was uncommunicative and looked ill, and Nona was quieter than usual, as well. She was, as always, working but, deep in thought, she observed her daughter and son-in-law and the children out of the corner of her eyes. They did not know what to think. Finally, Raeto asked his grandmother shyly whether they had done something wrong.

At that, Nona responded decisively, 'It is time that you learnt what has happened. It has nothing to do with you, but you have the right to know what is going on. Your father has lost his job — the construction company does not have enough work and therefore cannot keep everybody employed.'

Blankly, the children looked at their grandmother. They could not comprehend the significance of the situation, until Nona slowly and firmly added, 'Your father will be unemployed.'

That, on the other hand, the children understood, as there was talk of unemployment everywhere. The papers were full of it. In the village, news of individuals having lost their jobs did the rounds. Several families had moved away from St Moritz and they had to say goodbye to school friends. There were men who hid the fact that they had lost their work. Quietly and secretly, they had left town with their families as if the word 'unemployed' stuck to them like a blemish.

It was a shock for the children that their father, too, was now one of the unemployed. Nobody in the family had ever imagined that the renowned construction firm would be drawn into the vortex of the crisis and that their father, who had been working there for years, could lose his position.

Nina knew that the children spoke to each other about it, and she once overheard a conversation between the girls.

Marcella said optimistically, 'Father will find something, I am sure', but Anita responded precociously.

'I am not so sure; Papa is sixty soon, and you constantly hear that people who are that old hardly ever find work.'

It seemed to Nina as if they were in the same situation as when they had the difficulties with the house in Celerina, when she simply refused to give up and kept looking for solutions, but now she could not see a way out, however much she racked her brain. She succumbed to a paralysing desperation.

175

One day Maria declared resolutely, 'This cannot go on. We must not, under any circumstances, hang our heads. Somehow, life must go on.'

'But how? What can we do?' Nina asked quietly.

'I have thought about it. We cannot just wait; we have to do something. Is it shameful, after all, to lose one's job, particularly at this time, when more and more firms have to close? Surely anyone can be hit. Diethelm should write to all his friends and acquaintances and tell them that he is looking for a job. Nina, you can also look for work. You do not have to worry about the house. I shall move in with you. I am still healthy and will be able to cope with whatever there is to do. Perhaps we can try to open a guesthouse, just as we did in the past. Even though there are fewer holiday guests than previously, we could probably still earn some money. We would, of course, have to have a bigger apartment closer to the centre.'

Nina and Diethelm were sceptical. Where was there work for Diethelm and where for Nina? Where could an apartment be found that was not too expensive? Maria was not to be deterred and managed to convince her daughter and son-in-law that everything must be tried. The two of them had little hope, but still responded positively to Maria's suggestions, and Nina even dared to put a job-seeking advertisement into the newspaper.

A stranger's voice in an unknown language made Anita embarrassed when she picked up the telephone. She was still confused when she fetched her father, who had just come home. She heard how he repeatedly answered 'yes' in English and saw how his face lit up. He slowly put the receiver onto the hook next to the telephone on the wall and went into the kitchen to talk to Nina.

'I have been offered the job of Secretary of the St Moritz Bobsleigh Club', he said.

Nina looked at him in astonishment.

'Who said that?'

'The President — Colonel Orr — you know him, too. We often had to deal with him when we were both working for St Moritz Tourism. He has just called and offered me the job.'

Nina could hardly believe it — Diethelm had found a position, what a stroke of luck. She knew, of course, that the work with the Bob Club was limited to the winter season, and clearly only lasted as long as the ice run for the bobsleighs was in operation. She also suspected that the salary would not match what he had earned previously, but was convinced that her mother and she would cope. They had, after all, a lot of practice.

'I can start on 1 December, before the notice period has expired, that is when work for the construction of the run has to begin and the programme and the events have to be organised', Diethelm added. The Christmas period was quieter for the family than usual. Candles were lit on the tree, as always, and there were presents, too: as normal, practical items which were useful in daily life — clothes, shoes, school material. And there was no lack of books, either: Christmas without books would have been unimaginable.

The near future was taken care of, even if they had to cut back more than in the past. Admittedly — his work for the Bob Club would finish by the end of April at the latest. When the bob run could not be used any more in March, there were still some administrative tasks to be done and the books had to be balanced, but it was obvious that after that, there was an end even to clerical tasks.

Father Christmas had brought the children new skis, which had to be tested in front of the house at the edge of the forest

At that stage, though, they moved into their new home. Acting on Maria's advice, Nina had looked for a larger apartment and — lo and behold — had found one with more rooms and in a central position.

The move took place on a sunny spring day. Saying farewell to the house on the stream, where they had spent such a happy time, was not only difficult for Nina, but also for Diethelm and Maria, and even for the children. As is normal with children, however, they were full of curiosity and looking forward to all the new adventures that lay ahead.

When the midday bell tolled, the last basket was unloaded from the cart, and the carriage and pair started to move on again, clattering towards the village. Nina followed them from her window. She saw Marcella on the dusty road below, raising her hand as if to wave goodbye, but then letting it fall with such a tired, resigned gesture that Nina realised that her daughter had taken in the significance of this change. Her childhood was over. Never again would she build dams in the brook to create little ponds to do her dolls' laundry, never again look for strawberries in the little forest over there, nor observe birds and squirrels. She would no longer take the interesting, varied path to school between pine and larch trees, which brought her to the country road leading to the school — everything would be different. Indeed, the serious side of life had arrived very fast for her children. They had to grow up, help, take responsibility, make sure that they made progress both at school and in the world of work. Gone was the time of playing, dreaming and endless reading.

That first summer was not easy. Total commitment was needed from all of them. Some small businesses employed Diethelm by the hour to do some administrative work, but that neither provided sufficient money, nor guaranteed a regular income. They felt optimistic, however, about the letting of their guest rooms in the new apartment, even though prices had to be set low. All the more, Nina appreciated the writing jobs and the temporary secretarial work she was asked to do, which supplemented their rather low earnings.

Maria had given up her post as manager of laundry and linen in the Hotel Cresta Kulm at the end of the winter season and had completely moved in with Nina's family. With few personal belongings — among them her great-grandmother's spinning wheel and the silk shawl — she installed herself in the smallest room of the new apartment. The children, too, had taken on temporary holiday jobs during the long summer vacations.

Fortunately, winter brought improvements. Diethelm could start his job with the St Moritz Bobsleigh Club again in November, and the horse racing club,[30] which organised the big events on the frozen lake, appointed Nina as full-time secretary for the winter season. At home, Maria was in charge: she looked after and catered for the guests who had rented the three rooms. Not enough to make great strides, as Nina observed to herself, but sufficient to get by.

The following summer, coping on such meagre incomes was a matter of touch and go, and this caused Nina to have sleepless nights. She felt responsible for the very survival of the family, for her old mother, for her husband — now more than sixty years old — and, of course, for the future of her children. The thought of their education and what this would inevitably cost did not leave her.

She was, however, grateful and aware how kind fate had been to them so far, how much solidarity the family had

---

[30] This club is now called 'White Turf'; it still organises flat, trotting and skijöring races on Lake St Moritz every winter.

been shown by their fellow citizens in the village, and how people had remembered Diethelm and her when job vacancies arose. To be despondent was not in her nature, but she wanted to believe, just like Maria, that 'a little window would always open again'.

'We have to talk about your professional future', Nina said one evening, when the family was sitting around the kitchen table. She had known for a long time that Raeto was dreaming of a technical career, if possible in the area of machine engineering. It was not possible to be trained in engineering in a region as remote as the Engadin. He would therefore, like her brother Rudolf when he was young, have to find an apprenticeship in the lower part of Switzerland and pay for accommodation and food. How could she raise the necessary funds to cover these costs and raise the money needed for an apprenticeship away from home? They had managed to muddle through so far, but had lived from hand to mouth — no other major expenses were possible. And it was not only Raeto, of course — the two daughters should also learn a profession.

It would have been wrong to close one's eyes and ignore these problems, and for this reason, she presented her loved ones with the facts as she saw them, bluntly. There were funds for only one of the three to continue their education.

With one voice, Anita and Marcella said, 'It must be Raeto, of course. He should be able to embark on the career he is keen on, and that can obviously only happen in the lower part of Switzerland. Do not worry, we shall somehow manage and make our own way.'

'You, too, need a proper occupation', Nina pointed out. 'You see yourselves how important it is that I can work as a professional. Papa and I therefore want you get a degree from the commercial college, which we are fortunate to have in St Moritz. We can afford the additional cost of sending you to school for longer, as you can live at home. This will certainly be possible, particularly now that I have a job in the technical office of the President of the Horse Racing Club during the summer.'

The two girls looked at each other. Commercial high school, in that case. This was exactly what suited Anita; Nina knew that. Marcella, on the other hand, was more of a linguist and she probably had different dreams, but the local commercial college was the only chance for them to broaden their education, and Nina was not really in any doubt that Marcella would accept this opportunity. She was greatly relieved when both immediately agreed to this plan.

The family in 1935

'For sale — private boarding house in St Moritz — owner retiring.' Diethelm entered the kitchen, with the newspaper advertisement in his hand. Dinner was over, and Nina and Maria were discussing meals and shopping plans for the next few days. A guest house? The two women looked at each other.

'Now, that might be something', Maria reckoned. 'We know this trade, do we not?'

Nina took the paper from her husband and studied the advert. It did not give much away. There was mention of it being in a central position, it had existing clientele, and fixtures and furniture would be included in the price. As Nina passed the paper on to her mother, she tried to imagine the sum that would be asked for the fittings and equipment. Discouraged, she shook her head. It would not work. Three years without a regular income had drained their savings so badly that the small amount they still had would probably not be enough for such a major expense. And she was about to say so, but Maria interrupted her.

'Try we must. You write to the box number at once. Then we know what is what, who is who, and how much they are asking, and after that we shall see.'

The same evening, Nina wrote the letter, and Mrs Caty, the owner of the guest house, called back within a week. She had been widowed early in life and this business had enabled her to bring up and educate her three children after the death of her husband. Her clients were, on the whole, young professionals who worked in the post office, in banks and in businesses; they had lodgings with families, but took their meals in a private pension in St Moritz. Mrs Caty ran her enterprise in a large rented apartment on the main road. Two spacious living rooms had been turned into dining rooms, where long tables could accommodate around thirty guests. There were two stoves in the large kitchen, an electric and a wood-burning one. The big kitchen table was used for the preparation of food. It was also the place where the family ate after the paying guests had been served.

Nina's heart was beating hard when, responding to Mrs Caty's invitation for a chat, she entered her apartment. She was informed that several people had expressed an interest. On the basis of her own personal experiences, she had decided in favour of the family with the unemployed father. Nina was so touched that she nearly burst into tears and only just managed to control her feelings sufficiently to understand Mrs Caty's explanations. The price charged for the inventory was, admittedly, a modest sum, but even so Nina did not know how to find that amount, given the scant savings they had available. However, the prospect of a possibly secure future made her almost excited and she accepted the proposal. Mrs Caty added that she had already talked to the owner of the house and he had agreed to let the apartment to Nina for use as a guest house, with effect from the end of September. Thus the deal was sealed.

Within a year, first Anita and then Marcella obtained their business diplomas. As was customary in a place where people from all over the world meet up, the next step was devoted to learning languages. Both girls found positions as au pairs with good families in Geneva and took language lessons with a student who was reading Romance languages and literature. They worked diligently on consolidating their school French and enjoyed the beautiful city on the lake, making the most of its rich culture.

They were quite surprised when they received their mother's letter telling them that she had — with the help of their grandmother — taken over Mrs Caty's boarding house. The move to the house on the main road would take place in the autumn. She expressed the hope that the family would have a secure existence.

When the girls returned from Geneva, their mother was the owner of a boarding house, and the tables in the two dining rooms were fully occupied during meal times. A young student apprentice was helping with the serving at lunch and dinner times, while Mamma and Nona were busy cooking in the kitchen. Raeto, who was in his last year at school, also lent a hand where necessary. Diethelm, who always got up early, helped with breakfast for those guests who had to be at work before 7 a.m. In addition, he dealt with the paperwork, but was still Secretary of the Bobsleigh Club during winter. There were fewer jobs for him during summer and he only worked sporadically, but the income from the boarding house was enough to cover the family's needs.

At last, Nina could breathe a sigh of relief. Anita joined the administrative department of a big sports shop, Marcella served the guests during meal times at home instead of the apprentice and, in addition, worked in a textile shop, paid by the hour. A year later, Raeto was able to achieve his dream and start his professional training in an engineering factory in the lower part of Switzerland.

Nina was investigating where her younger daughter could continue her education. This did not prove easy: all over Europe dark clouds were looming. As the political situation became increasingly threatening, tourism was badly affected, and the number of guests dropped. Nina was relieved to see that her boarding house continued to flourish. As far as Marcella was concerned, she wanted to improve her English, having learnt the basics at school for two years. They sought, and found, a position as an au pair. Just as Marcella's departure was imminent, Germany invaded Czechoslovakia and a telegram arrived from Great Britain announcing the annulment of all visas, including Marcella's. Her disappointment was immense. Nina would have been so happy if her daughter, who was such a keen linguist, had been able to go, but it was not to be. She asked Diethelm and Maria for advice. Which language, or which country, could be considered?

'How about Italian? That would be useful, too. Do you remember, Nina, how it was for you?' Diethelm interjected.

Indeed, that would certainly suit Marcella, but would it not be irresponsible to send such a young girl abroad in these uncertain times?

Her parents and grandmother deliberated at length.

'If only we could afford a college', Nina sighed. 'I would be much happier if I knew she was in a safe place, given the current circumstances, but that will no doubt cost too much.'

'Find out how much such a college would charge. The Italian currency is so low at the moment. Perhaps we could raise the amount for such a school — if possible, one close to the border', Maria said.

Nina looked at her mother slightly incredulously, but at the same time quickly began to estimate in her head her income and the potential costs for the college. She promised to investigate.

A boarding school in the Valtellina, not far away, was recommended and the offer the headmaster made was reasonable. In May, Marcella entered the convent school, San Lorenzo, in Sondrio. It would prove a most enriching time for her. She wrote home with great enthusiasm about the private lessons she had, because she was able to communicate in Italian, like everyone in the Engadin, but could not yet keep up with the native speakers among the students. She reported that the silence in the convent helped her work intensively and, although she was a Protestant herself, she found living with the Catholic nuns and their spirituality a very positive experience. All of this was exactly what she had wanted, as she was aware that one could not foresee how long she could remain in San Lorenzo and what the future would bring in this world, which had become so dark and sinister.

At the end of August 1939, alarm bells were ringing again all over Switzerland — another war. Suddenly only four of the thirty boarding house guests were sitting at the table. All healthy young men had to join up. Naturally, there was no question anymore of operating the bobsleigh in the winter. As a result, Diethelm had no work, even during the winter. Whether Anita would keep her job in the sports shop was also doubtful — who would need sports equipment now?

With a heavy heart Nina had to write to her daughter saying that she should make good use of her time, because during the winter season her help would be needed at home again. The budget would not stretch to employing outside help for the running of the boarding house.

Thus, Marcella returned at the end of November. Some of the boarders had been demobilised, as workers were needed for civilian duties. The relevant authorities introduced a rota system, according to which men in military service were taking turns with civilians, so that the country still functioned. This way, some sort of normal, everyday life began to return, albeit in a reduced fashion, particularly when it came to food. Rationing had been introduced and it was difficult to provide good nourishing meals with the scant allocations. However, Maria and Nina had experience. They had, after all, coped during the First World War.

187

Nina, Maria and Diethelm in 1935

The war would only last a few months — so everyone had thought. Following the German army's invasion of the Netherlands, Belgium and France in May 1940, nobody was in doubt that hard times were in store for all. Again, the men were enlisted. Only the few who were exempt from military service remained in the boarding house, so that Nina and Maria, with Anita, could cope with the work over lunchtime.

Friends who had a hotel in Davos, which was completely booked up with military personnel, sent a cry for help. Marcella moved to Davos to care for the owners' little child, and she also helped wherever else she was needed. This, too, turned out to be an instructive period for her, as she gained a useful insight into the running of a hotel.

Everyday life felt increasingly cramped in a country hemmed in by the Axis powers of Germany and Italy. Food rations were reduced, and heating, electricity, textiles, leather, soap and other goods were now also rationed. Making do with the small allocations for house guests and family caused Nina and Maria a lot of headaches. Thanks to their skill and creativity, however, they managed to feed the remaining guests to their satisfaction. The pension was not full, but given the circumstances, it was always reasonably busy.

Diethelm missed his winter job in the Secretariat of the Bobsleigh Club, and his other tasks had also disappeared. He made himself useful around the house wherever he could, but Nina was painfully aware that he was depressed at the thought of being a burden. If he did not have to carry heavy shopping home for the boarding house, he barely left home, and his cosmopolitan, interested manner had given way to a quiet resignation.

Diethelm happened to be crossing the main square in St Moritz, weighed down by two heavy shopping bags, when Giacomo, a good friend, stopped him. He was the commander of the air force monitoring office that had been set up at the time Swiss airspace was beginning to be frequently invaded by the warring nations. On occasion, bombs had been dropped on Swiss territory by accident. There were control towers along the border from where messages on the movements of foreign airplanes were sent to higher authorities to be analysed. Auxiliary and voluntary troops were deployed in these posts.

'We do not have enough people in our evaluation office', Giacomo said.

'Surely, I am too old', Diethelm remarked defensively.

'Rubbish! You are in amazing shape, given that you are sixty-five. Why do you not ask to have a medical examination like all troops have to undergo? Then you will find out.'

Diethelm could not quite believe that the army would accept him, but he enlisted anyway. The examination confirmed Giacomo's judgement, and Diethelm was declared fit. Now he had a purpose again, plus a small salary and, in addition, a refund for potential loss of earnings that all soldiers received. This way, the hole in the income from the guest house was partially filled.

There was a lot of snow in the sixth winter of the war. Even in March, the valley was under a deep white cover. The streets were barely cleared and only open to sledges. Thick flakes swirled through the air that evening when the doorbell rang after 9 p.m. Nina opened and was puzzled to see Paulin, the boy next door.

'What on earth are you doing at this time of night outside? What has happened?'

Paulin stuttered, embarrassed, 'Do you have some cigarette coupons by any chance?'

Like everything else, tobacco was also rationed. Everyone received a monthly ration card, which contained a stamp for tobacco. As nobody in Nina's family smoked, these coupons were a popular — if actually illegal — means of barter. Smokers sometimes exchanged them for their food coupons.

Nina shook her head and said harshly, 'You surely know full well that you are not allowed to smoke.'

'But I do not want the cigarettes for myself', Paulin said, nearly crying, 'they are for the poor refugees in the street outside.'

A few more explanations were needed, before Nina understood, but then she went quickly and fetched the stamps and went outside with Paulin. She would never forget the scene that awaited her there. There was a group of people in rags, guarded by soldiers. On a low sled, there were three more figures, cowering. Their clothes were pitiful. They had wrapped themselves in old thin covers, which they had pulled over their heads, so that their faces were barely visible. Their feet were swathed in sacks. The poor people were shivering with cold. Some of the villagers who were standing around ran back into their houses and returned with articles of clothing and warmer blankets.

Nina, too, wanted to return to her house, to fetch warm things, when Paulin grabbed her hand and said to her forcefully, 'They want cigarettes. Look, the shop is open, but without stamps the store is not allowed to give them cigarettes.'

Indeed, the tobacconist's was open. Nina gave the shopkeeper her stamps and received several packets of cigarettes, which she distributed among the refugees. More and more villagers turned up, some with thermos flasks and hot drinks, some with bread and other food. Suddenly, one of the huddled figures raised himself on the sled and staggered to his feet, only to collapse into the snow with a sigh. Bystanders helped him get back onto the sled. The doctor, who lived next door, was called and began a medical examination by the weak, bluish light of a torch. The doctor lifted his head at once and looked into the silent crowd.

'This is a woman. She has been injured; there are three bullet holes in her shoulder.'

People were clearly horrified, judging by the expressions on their faces, but then everything happened very quickly.

An old wood-gas vehicle was requisitioned to transport the woman to hospital. Two more refugees, who could obviously not take any more, were loaded into the car too, and they departed. The tension slowly eased and people started to talk to each other. The rest of the refugees belonged to a group of Italian partisans in the mountains who were fighting the German occupiers. A massive contingent of the Waffen-SS had been deployed to attack them so that they had to withdraw ever higher up into the wintry mountains. In the end, they found themselves surrounded and had only just managed to escape to Switzerland over the ridge of the mountains.

'What! In this snow, they got over the steep rocks into the Val Bregaglia?' someone shouted. 'And what next?'

'Then we climbed down into the valley; I do not know how. At the bottom we were half dead.'

'And you walked from the Val Bregaglia to here?'

'We could only get hold of this sled', one of the soldiers explained. 'This way everyone was able to ride at least for a bit of the way. We took turns. Now the weakest can sit on the sled. We have to go on, to the reception centre.'

He signalled, and the sad group went on in the direction of Samedan.

Incidents like these were signs of increased activity by the resistance in the conquered neighbouring countries, and at the same time, of course, of the increasingly harsh response by the German occupiers. Even so, they represented a silver lining on the horizon; the hope for an end to the war.

The desire and will to start rebuilding stirred cautiously. Tourism St Moritz, too, prepared to pick up its previous activities again. Marcella was asked whether she would be interested in a job like the one her mother had had years ago. Nina knew at once that this was the big chance for her daughter. Admittedly, she would have to be replaced in the family business, so extra help would have to be employed there.

Again, Nina sat over figures and accounts, calculated, and consulted with Diethelm and Maria. It had to work out. A girl from the neighbouring village could be hired as an assistant. The efficient and hardworking Cilgia eagerly threw herself into the job and became a personal friend to all.

For Marcella, it was the beginning of a new era, which opened up a wealth of new experiences and adventures. Nina was very happy to see her daughter enjoy what had previously been her own tasks and responsibilities as much as she had done herself in the past.

Peace in Europe — at long last. In celebration, the bells chimed throughout the whole country on this memorable day, 8 May 1945. Nina stood in the spring sun on their roof terrace with Diethelm and her mother. The five bells of the nearby church tower were ringing harmoniously just a few steps away. People could be heard rejoicing down below in the street. Deep in thought, Diethelm gazed at the swifts that were shooting past under a silk-blue sky.

'This very day they have arrived', he said. 'Is it really over, all this fighting and killing? All this bombardment and destruction?'

All three had now experienced a world war for the second time, and again their country had been spared. What a miracle, what mercy! In silence, they leaned against the wall of the staircase. They did not feel jubilant, but full of respect and reverence — overwhelming sentiments that made them quiet and which would have been violated if words had been uttered. Tremendously moved, they became lost in reminiscences of their long lives and knew that, at this hour, gratitude was the only appropriate feeling.

Admittedly, many months passed before the borders with the countries that surrounded Switzerland were opened up again, and even longer before tourism slowly recovered. Nevertheless, the number of lodgers increased once more.

The air force monitoring centre was closed down in the summer and Diethelm lost not only the job that had given him much satisfaction, but also the income that had helped them survive with fewer lodgers. Although he was now nearly seventy, he missed having a task, and that bothered him. He began to feel unwell. A medical examination discovered bladder cancer. Surgery gave hope that he would improve, but it was obvious that his strength was declining.

The table in the boarding house was fully occupied again. Maria, who was over eighty by now, would not have been able to exist without a purpose in life and thus continued to help in the kitchen. Some of the guests had formed a group who hiked in the mountains in their spare time. Duri, an enthusiastic and experienced alpinist, used to be their leader. He was a carpenter and worked in a fairly large firm. Whenever possible, Marcella joined the group. It was obvious from the way her eyes shone when she told her family about these excursions, and when she talked about the joys of being outdoors, pushing herself hard to test her limits.

Naturally, Nina noticed that, as time went by, these were not the only factors that counted, but that being with Duri was as important to Marcella. He, too, wanted to be close to her daughter, and every now and then he sat with the family in the kitchen of an evening. It therefore did not come as a surprise when on such an occasion they mentioned a future together.

Maria in 1950   Duri in 1945

'Ah, that is how it goes', she interrupted one of those conversations, 'and you have not even asked us.'

'Let us do it now, in that case', Duri responded quickly, 'or am I expected to turn up dressed to perfection and submit a formal proposal as was customary in the past?'

Diethelm smiled.

'We shall accept this style as sufficient.'

They would have a conventional engagement party, not a big event though, because Diethelm had become very weak. In the presence of parents and grandmother, Duri and Marcella exchanged rings on a Sunday in November.

Diethelm died only a few weeks later. For Nina it was the end of her world. He had been a loyal, loving and affectionate husband to her throughout their marriage. They had experienced happy years together and they had shared difficult times.

He had always been attentive and kind to her mother too, and for the children he had been an understanding and tolerant father who, with his versatility and openness to the world, had provided them with a profound knowledge of life and the world. They had dreamt of a time that would not only consist of daily struggles, but would allow them to enjoy quiet years in peaceful contemplation.

She felt miserable and drained, and her own health also suffered a terrible sudden decline. It was discovered that she, too, had cancer. She took a long time to recover after surgery. The boarding business fortunately continued as usual, thanks to the total commitment of Maria, Cilgia and Marcella, who had been able to reduce her hours with St Moritz Tourism after her marriage to Duri and lived just a few steps away from the family's guest house.

The candles on the Christmas tree radiated their soft light in Duri's and Marcella's cosy living room, as they were sitting at the table with Maria and Nina and exchanged gifts.

'We have saved you a big present — it will only be delivered in the summer', Duri said, and glanced mischievously at his wife — 'something special for grand- and great-grandmothers.'

Nina and Maria looked quizzically at the young ones, whose sparkling eyes quickly gave the secret away.

'A baby? You will have a baby?'

In August, Marcella had a girl, who was christened Tina. This new young life restored Nina's energy. Marcella visited them every day with her 'Poppina', as Maria and Nina tenderly called the child in Romansh. After two years, another little daughter arrived, Corina, and these children brought a lot of sunshine into the daily grind and gave Nina a new lease of life. It felt as if one ring was joining another to form a chain through the generations of these women, showing the way from the distant past to the future, and these thoughts filled Nina with joy and gratitude.

Raeto, who was working in a factory in the lower parts of Switzerland after he had graduated, delighted his mother with frequent visits. He often mentioned that a spell abroad would be professionally important for him, but Nina did not take much notice of this, even when there was occasional talk of South America. It was therefore unexpected when he declared on his next visit home, 'I have been offered a managerial position in a large business in São Paulo, Brazil. This is an exceptional opportunity and I have been shortlisted because one of my old professors recommended me.'

This was hard for Nina. Her devoted son would live so far away — how long would it be until they saw each other again? Would he ever return, or would he stay abroad?

'This is such a stroke of luck for Raeto', Anita said. She, and Marcella as well, appreciated how hard this separation would be for their mother, but they both encouraged her to support the plan.

'Let him go', they said, 'otherwise he will regret not having taken up this offer and will always feel that his future has been ruined.'

Shortly before his departure, Anita, who had a good position in a factory on Lake Zurich, which produced school furniture, married. Her husband, Walter, was a widower and had a young daughter, Annemarie, whose attachment to Anita and to her relatives in St Moritz would always mean a great deal to all of them.

The line of women has continued to the sixth generation: Maria with her great-granddaughter Tina in the centre, with Marcella on the left and Nina on the right

Duri and Marcella's apartment, situated directly on the main road, which saw the volume of traffic continuously increase, was not good for the children. A different solution had to be found. There was a possibility of renting a flat below the main part of the village, near the train station and the lake. It was in a sunny, detached house with big, bright rooms, a terrace and a garden surrounded by mountain pines, birch and rowan trees.

In October, they moved into the house, which was called 'Chesa Spelma'. In their new home, the youngsters had a happy childhood with a lot of free space, which stimulated their imaginations and creativity in many different ways. The lively group of children in the Chesa Spelma and in the wider neighbourhood hatched the most amazing plots and lived to see the most marvellous adventures together.

The mountain slopes on the other side of the valley were still covered in snow, but there were already yellow and purple crocuses in the garden, planted by Duri on the edge of the vegetable beds in the autumn. A blackbird was warbling its spring tunes on the top of the pine tree. While Corina slept peacefully in her cot on the terrace, Tina was busy watering the flower pots, which her mother had put outdoors, with her little can.

'You will have to come and see the garden; it is turning green and the first flowers are already in bloom', Marcella enthused when she, as always, dropped in on her mother and grandmother on her return from shopping in town.

St Moritz in the 1950s. The Chesa Spelma is visible on the very right of the picture, second house from the right, above the train track

Nina, who lived in the centre of the village, still missed the proximity to nature, and promised to make a visit to inspect the garden, while Maria felt that making her way to the Chesa Spelma would be too exhausting. She was over eighty by now, her eyesight was failing, and this meant a considerable reduction in the quality of life, particularly as she had always been very active. She could not see well enough to help with the cooking. As everything that appeared on the table of a guesthouse had to be immaculate, there was no way she could contribute during this stage of food preparation, nor could she be expected to wash the dishes properly or assist with other tasks in the kitchen. Little accidents happened to her and her hands were no longer as nimble and agile as they had once been. This made her impatient and dissatisfied, sometimes even gloomy, as she felt that she was no longer needed.

Nina, who had come to admire the garden, sat on the bench next to the fountain and talked to Duri and Marcella about this unhappy situation.

'I feel sorry when I see Nona so unhappy, but you know that a restaurant has strict health and safety regulations when it comes to cleanliness and I cannot risk complaints from my guests. I do not know how to solve the problem, as Mamma cannot bear sitting around with nothing to do.'

'Why does she not come to live with us?' Duri asked. 'We have enough space; the little room is free for the time being. There is always something to do in the house, and there is no need for anything to be perfect. Moreover, she will get on very well with the children.'

Marcella thought this was an excellent suggestion, but Nina hesitated — could she really burden the younger generation with her old mother just like that? And would Maria agree?

It was thanks to Duri's and Marcella's powers of persuasion that Nina could be convinced, and to everyone's surprise, Maria also stopped objecting. Thus, the great-grandmother, known as 'Tatta' in Romansh, moved into the Chesa Spelma where she found a role in the household and with childcare, which gave her much joy. When the children had been put to bed after an early dinner, she sat with Duri and Marcella and talked about her own long life, as well as those of her mother and grandmother.

Raeto had returned home from Brazil for the first time after five years. He had hardly changed and was still the unpretentious and warm son, touchingly devoted to his mother. Just then, Duri and Marcella were given the opportunity to purchase their house, on the condition that they make a quick decision.

'Grab it, grab it at once', Raeto said. 'You must not miss such a chance. If necessary, I shall contribute, because this is exactly what I have been wanting for Mamma — an apartment near you. It is time that she gave up her exhausting boarding house business. To know that she and our Nona, too, are cared for in their old age, would reassure me a great deal.'

Apart from the short deadline, this was just about the perfect solution, particularly as there was a large, empty room in the basement suitable for a carpenter to establish a carpentry workshop. And this had been Duri's dream for a long time. Although financing proved to be a problem, Duri and Marcella took the risk of buying the house and set up their own carpentry. The first years were hard, as the house needed considerable renovation. Fortunately, the business was a success and they managed to make ends meet, if only just.

With regard to the purchase of the Chesa Spelma, Raeto pointed out that the strenuous and long days in the boarding house might soon prove to be beyond Nina's strength — he felt she should start thinking about retirement. The thought had occurred to Nina herself and she repeatedly grappled with the idea, notably because she was starting to suffer from health problems, not from anything serious, but she caught colds ever more often and then could not shake them off for many weeks. Standing in the kitchen for such long periods badly affected her legs; they were so painful that they stopped her from sleeping. She could not conceal these problems from herself — she was starting to feel the symptoms of old age.

When she talked about this with her son-in-law Duri, he also thought that her ill health was a sign that it was time to give up her business and to plan a more leisurely lifestyle. It would be easy for her to move into one of the smaller apartments, which were currently rented out.

Nina replied that she would be overjoyed to live under the same roof with her daughter's family, all the more as the two granddaughters, Tina and Corina, were already going to Kindergarten and she had not really been able to enjoy them properly when they were smaller. Duri agreed that she had indeed missed out in that respect.

'We could of course make up for lost time', he said with a mischievous smile. 'If you decide to give up your professional life, I may perhaps post another letter.'

Only after Duri had left her flat, did it dawn on Nina what he had meant by the weird phrase 'posting a letter'. In any case, she felt reinforced in her decision to go into retirement now. Marcella and he were obviously considering having another child.

And this was, indeed, how things turned out. Nina gave up the business, but at first kept her flat in the centre of the village. In the autumn, exactly on Corina's birthday, her daughter's family welcomed their third girl, Seraina, into the world.

They were a cheerful and lively family, and Nina, who was now free to decide how to spend her time, made up for what she had missed with her granddaughters in the past and visited them frequently. She often marvelled that the turbulent everyday life was not too much for her old mother. This thought, however, could only make the old mother herself smile — children had always been her great joy. The great-grandmother was adored by the little ones; she always had time for them, took them into her arms, cuddled them, played with them and told them the most beautiful stories.

Just as if fate had decided, an apartment in the Chesa Spelma became vacant in the spring. The elderly couple who lived on the same floor as Marcella's family moved to another village and the decision for Nina was therefore easy. Nothing stood in the way of the move into the children's house any more. The apartment was on the south side, and it was spacious and sunny. There was a cosy living room with larch panelling, a large porch, which Nina turned into her bedroom and study, with a desk and her beloved typewriter. Another room was available for her mother. In addition, there was a modern bathroom and a bright kitchen.

As soon as Nina had arranged everything, Maria wanted to move in there. Nina already envisaged herself sitting at the big window with the view onto the beautiful mountain scenery and the magnificent forests. How she was looking forward to this vista over the lake, with the thousand stars sparkling on the waves in spring and the sailing boats gliding across the water in the summer.

View from the Chesa Spelma toward the Rosatsch massif

The most beautiful time was autumn, however, when the clear mirror of the lake reflected the image of the valley opposite with the luminous yellow larch trees and snow-covered peaks. Winter announced itself with a light fog rising out of the water, which was turning cooler, ice starting to form. At night, the lake seemed to fight against being locked in with loud howls, groans and noisy crunching, until the long silence began, when the snow fell in dense flakes and covered the transparent black ice with a thick, white coat.

On a sunny day in early spring, Duri and Nina unpacked Maria's belongings into the cupboard of the freshly renovated room. From now on, mother and daughter would share a home, and both were looking forward to it.

Nina stood at the window and looked at the first wild tulips and crocuses, which were in bloom right outside the house. On the first green blades of the lawn, the sparrows were chirping harmoniously. Maria, who was putting her underwear into the chest of drawers, joined them. She held the green silk shawl, which had belonged to her grandmother in the Val Bregaglia.

'Now you shall have it, the fourth in the line of us women.'

Just like Alma in her day, Nina weighed the cloth in her hand, unfurled it and was astonished that there was no crease even though it had been stored tightly folded.

'To which of my two daughters should I pass it on to?' Nina asked.

Before Maria could answer, Duri rushed in. He was carrying Don Gerolamo's spinning wheel and was looking around trying to find a place for it.

'It will fit perfectly in the corner, here, near the window. What do you think, Tatta, will one of our girls one day learn how to work with it?'

Deep in thought Maria looked at the wheel.

'Yes, my grandmother at the spinning wheel — how many years have passed since I was with her in Soglio. I can picture her, working and telling me stories about her life. And now I have grown so old. I can barely believe that I am over ninety.' Switching into her native Romansh, she added, 'Uoss'es ura, cha'l Segner lascha giò chavagna.' ('Time has come for God to lower the basket.')

Deep in thought, she laid her hand on the beautifully turned wheel and gave it a gentle push, which made it twirl effortlessly, just as she had seen it as a child, when she had stood next to the grandmother, way back on summer evenings in the tall house in Soglio.

Only three weeks later, Maria fell ill with pneumonia. With her usual determination, she declared that she had to go to hospital. Nina and Marcella tried in vain to convince her that caring for her at home was no trouble and that the doctor would make daily visits, and they assumed she would soon recover. Maria would not countenance objections and was taken to hospital in Samedan.

Marcella and the six-year-old Corina visited her the next morning. During the warm welcome, the grandmother held onto Marcella's hand with a firm squeeze, but after a while the pressure decreased, her eyelids closed, and her breathing became weaker, until it fell silent altogether. It was totally still in the room. Quietly, the child's voice could be heard on the windowsill, where Corina sat.

'Tatta is asleep now, is she not?'

'Yes, she is, and she is in paradise', whispered Marcella.

Don Gerolamo's spinning wheel, which accompanied the women

Raeto returned from Brazil in the same year and married Doris, a girl he had met whilst on holiday at home. The fact that he would now stay in Switzerland somewhat soothed the pain of her mother's death for Nina. A year later, Marcella's fourth daughter, Flurina, was born and only two days later, Raeto's wife had a son.

The years that followed were contented and peaceful for Nina. After the hectic life of running a boarding house, she enjoyed spending time quietly and tranquilly, free from the constant pressure of time. She did not wish to be idle, either, however — she was too much like her mother and her ancestors before her. She was determined to remain independent, ran her household alone, cooked for herself and ate her food next to the window in her kitchen. Occasionally, she invited one of the grandchildren for a meal, and sometimes she was, in turn, asked to join the table of her daughter's family. She enjoyed being on her own in the silence of her own four walls. Now she could do the things for which there had been no time over the last few years. In particular, reading had always been something of a luxury in the past, whereas now she could immerse herself in a newspaper, devote herself to books, whenever she felt like it, or listen to good music and interesting talks on the radio. It gave her great pleasure to sew and knit beautiful clothes for her granddaughters, and she loved seeing all four of them in identical pretty dresses.

At times, Nina could let the room that had been her mother's. That way she got to know widely travelled and cultured people, who over the years returned to spend their holidays with her. Raeto and his family were always particularly welcome. Ruedi, the oldest, had been joined by two girls, Claudia and Ursina.

Marcella and Duri in 1962

This happy time was cruelly interrupted by Raeto's sudden death. He died at the age of forty-six of appendicitis, which had not been diagnosed in time. Nina endured this heavy blow with admirable courage. It was touching how strongly Raeto's wife and his children were attached to their grandmother and they managed to fill the gap that their father's death had caused by spending their holidays as often as possible with Nina.

Old friends from Celerina visited Nina from time to time, among them Battista, an old school friend. When he noticed on one such occasion that she was working at her typewriter, he asked astonished whether it was now polite to write personal letters on a machine.

Nina laughed. 'Why ever not? Nowadays this is no longer impolite. Moreover, I am writing to Augusta, who went to school with us, as you know. She suffers from bad eyesight and finds it easier to read typed documents.'

'You write to her in Romansh?'

'Of course — this is also how we speak to each other.'

He hesitated a bit before he asked, 'Could you write letters in Romansh for me?'

'Yes, certainly. I still enjoy work that involves writing.'

'You will know that my family has several firms in Italy with which I am associated. I am in constant contact with the relatives who run these businesses and act as consultant to them. There is often paperwork to be dealt with, in Romansh when we correspond directly, in Italian when matters go via third persons or authorities. People complain that my handwriting is hard to decipher. Would you work with me on the Romansh and Italian correspondence, and possibly also the German documents?'

'Sure. I have enough time. Dealing with paperwork was, after all, my profession. It would give me great pleasure to take this up again.'

This way Nina found a new task, which provided enjoyment and satisfaction. As a result, it gave her courage to take on Romansh–German translations, and every now and then she even dared to write a newspaper article.

Nina took an active and close interest in how her grandchildren were growing up, enjoyed helping with homework, took great delight in good grades, and consoled them when something had gone wrong. She did not know boredom. Reading, writing, looking after her small household, crafts, the 'women's association' and the 'seniors' club' — all these interests and engagements filled her days. On beautiful summer days, she loved sitting under the lilac tree in the garden, inhaling the sweet fragrance from the white blossom.

On her 85th birthday, the village music society serenaded her. Flowers filled the house and the birthday cards grew into a large heap. She thanked each of the senders personally in writing.

In the months following her birthday, her health began to deteriorate. She felt her time had come and began to let go gently. She was bedbound for only a few weeks, cared for lovingly by her daughters and daughter-in-law.

One morning, shortly before Christmas, Marcella took something to drink to her mother and plumped up her pillow. She then intended to return to her own apartment to prepare breakfast for her family, but she felt a force that made her stay with Nina and hold her hand firmly. In astonishment and awe, she observed how her mother's wide open eyes became ever bigger and radiant. She entrusted herself with a saintly smile to her creator.

Four little girls, Marcella's daughters, from left to right:
Corina, Seraina, Flurina and Tina under the pine trees in the garden

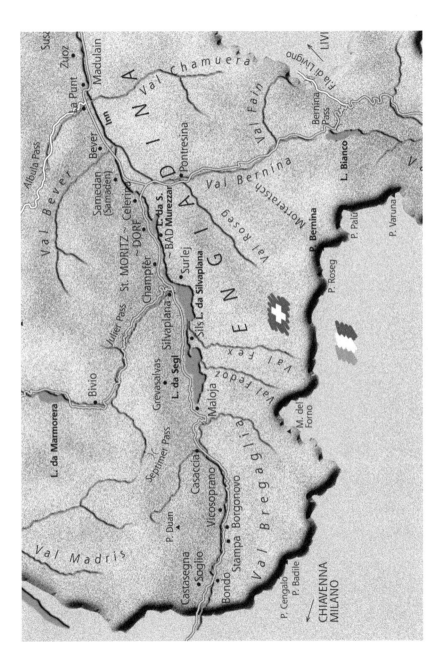

Register of persons

Val Bregaglia

Alma (1797–1877)   Lived in Bondo, later in Soglio in the Val Bregaglia

Don Gerolamo   Italian priest who was given refuge by Alma

Giovanni   Alma's husband

Lisabetta (1831–1913)   Alma's daughter

Soglio

Signora Anna   Alma's employer, owner of the Palazzo

Caterina   Signora Anna's maidservant

Giuliano   Farmer, Signora Anna's neighbour

Sils

Plasch   Lisabetta's husband

Sar Pol   Owner of a farm and later a guest house

Duonna Berta	Sar Pol's wife
Lorenzo	Sar Pol's son
Duonna Carla	Lorenzo's wife
Annetta	Sar Pol's daughter
Maria (1867–1957)	Lisabetta's daughter
Gian/Gianin	Lisabetta's son

Silvaplana

Anna-Barbla	Landlady of the hotel 'Wilder Mann'
Vicky	Anna-Barbla's daughter
Padruot	Maria's husband
Nina (1890–1975)	Maria's daughter
Rudolf	Maria's son
Dr Bernhard	Doctor in the Engadin valley and in the hospital in the Upper Engadin

Celerina

Giuditta, Alma, Annetta	Sisters who own the house Maria rents
Pierina	Washer woman

St Moritz

Sar Alfred	President of St Moritz Tourism
Diethelm	Nina's husband
Anita, Marcella, Raeto	Nina's children
Duri	Marcella's husband
Tina, Corina, Seraina, Flurina	Marcella's daughters

Photo credits

Marcella Maier: pages 39, 141, 156, 167, 174, 178, 182, 188, 195, 198, 204, 206, 208, 210

Dokumentationsbibliothek St. Moritz: pages 56, 67, 88, 109, 117, 138, 199

Eidgenössisches Amt für Denkmalspflege (EAD Bern): page 98 (EAD-Zin 66-1638-fp)

Rhätisches Museum, Chur: page 12 (H 1963.646), 00 (H 1965.725)